The Little Book

Thomas Clough

TABLE OF CONTENTS

Prologue 1

Chapter 1

Meet Harry Hay…………………………………….. 3

Chapter 2

Imaginary Minorities: The Anorexia Analogy……. 11

Chapter 3

Gays Against Gay Marriage ………………………... 19

Chapter 4

The Threat to True Marriage ………………………... 23

Chapter 5

Gay Liars and Liberal Idiots ……………………… 35

Chapter 6

Why Gays Fail the Minority Standard ……………. 39

Chapter 7

Homophobia ……………………………………… 45

Chapter 8

Setting the Stage for One-Sex Wedlock ………….57

Chapter 9

The Gay Agenda 69

Chapter 10

Still Crazy After All These Years 83

Chapter 11

Are Gays *Really* Just Like Black People? 95

Chapter 12

The Case Against One-Sex Wedlock 101

Chapter 13

Experiments in Gay Marriage Go Haywire 105

Chapter 14

Answering Andrew Sullivan...........................119

Chapter 15

Deflating Gay Fantasies 125

Chapter 16

A Few Words About Polygamy 131

Chapter 17

Gays Trash the Moral Matrix 137

Chapter 18

The Gay Agenda Goes to College 147

Chapter 19

The Arrogance of the Self Anointed 155

Chapter 20

Gays in the Workplace 163

Chapter 21

What Is to Be Done? 173

Author's Note:

The Little Book includes candid quotations, gay slang and graphic accounts of gay health issues and behaviors.

Thomas Clough is the author of **Weird Republic**, a collection of twenty essays from his website of the same name. He is also an award winning realist painter, a political cartoonist, an essayist and a member of American Mensa.

For gay Will W.

whose provocative interrogations

sparked this reply.

Prologue

This little book has one big ambition: to unmask the false history and political stagecraft that are the essence of the Gay Power phenomenon. Not so long ago the ninety-nine percent of Americans who were natural-born heterosexuals shared the common wisdom that homosexuals were "different" in ways that were problematic and challenging to heterosexual culture. Normal human beings understood that a single encounter with a homosexual could derail a normal youngster's chances of a happy life – a truism later confirmed by the thousands of heart-breaking testimonies of the victims of gay predation.

The horrible clergy scandal exploded in the midst of a lavishly-financed campaign by homosexual activists to convince us that the Boy Scouts of America was a hate group because it did not allow openly homosexual scout masters to take our sons off into the woods. When the clergy scandal broke, the homosexuals instantly fell silent about the Scouts and shifted their efforts to other battlefronts. It was then that the gays invented the myth of "pedophile priests" to explain away the horror of what average homosexuals had done to tens of thousands of young men. The bright line that defines pedophilia is *puberty* – not the age of consent. The fact that almost all of the victims of gay clergymen were past the age of puberty is proof beyond doubt that their homosexual victimizers were not pedophiles, but average gays.

My boyhood friends and I shared cautionary notes on how to avoid these creepy people. Not all of my friends were successful. Back then homosexuals were more socially isolated and less sophisticated than they are today. Back then homosexuals openly rhapsodized about the thrills of "man-boy love." Homosexuals were the vocal vanguard of an effort to abolish every age-of-consent law. Back then the contesting interests of homosexuals and the ninety-nine percent of normal humanity were clearly understood.

The spectacular rise of homosexuality from its ancient status as a marginal sexual quirk to the rank of being a new "alternative normal" that demands co-equal status to heterosexuality has happened within my lifetime. This rise of the gays is not the result of any healthy evolution in the average person's perception of homosexuality; it is the consequence of a cleverly scripted, well-coordinated and lavishly financed propaganda campaign.

This little book shines a light on the cynical gay-power media campaign that now shapes every gay-friendly newscast, newspaper article, movie and television script that you have ever been exposed to. It all began one summer evening in a California kitchen in 1948, when I was three years old.

Chapter One

Meet Harry Hay

There was a time when homosexuals weren't always in our faces, announcing their *needs*. There was a time when homosexuals kept their quirks hidden. That was before Harry Hay.

Six decades ago, Harry founded a secret organization called the Mattachine Society. Its name was derived from a medieval French term for male dancers who sometimes satirized social customs while dressed only in masks. Harry was a visionary; he sought to organize American homosexuals around the notion that they were an oppressed minority, like black people, who should agitate for homosexual "rights." He began in Los Angeles in 1950, at a time when virtually no one identified himself publicly as a homosexual.

Two years earlier, in 1948, Harry Hay was middle-aged and living with his wife, Anita Platsky, whom he had married to conceal his homosexuality. Harry was an ardent Communist, an aspiring actor and a disaffected Catholic. One summer night in '48 Harry attended an all-male party in L.A. and ruminated aloud about whether the Progressive Party candidate for president, Henry Wallace, might include a sexual privacy plank in his platform in return for the support of homosexuals. That night, while his wife and two adopted daughters slept, Harry scribbled the gay movement's first political manifesto with its organizing notion that gays were an oppressed minority. Harry's first choice was to call his group Bachelors Anonymous. It took him more than two years to recruit four other male homosexuals. Two of them had been Communist Party members; the third, Dale Jennings, was arrested the following year for soliciting sex from a policeman. The fourth man was Harry's lover, a Viennese immigrant named Rudi Gernreich, who would later become renowned (notorious?) as the designer of the topless bathing suit for women. Harry's Mattachine Society hired a lawyer to defend Dale Jennings against the solicitation charge, claiming police entrapment, and won an acquittal.

The *New York Times* published an obituary of Harry Hay on October 25, 2002 that ran for 35 column inches. This was followed by a glowing article about Harry on October 30th and yet another in the choice Sunday magazine section of the *Times* on December 29th. The *Times* couldn't tell us enough about Harry Hay, the founder of gay liberation, who had died at age 90. These fawning articles pretty much covered Harry's entire life, including his anti-draft and anti-war activities during the Second World War. The *Times* even made mention of Harry's participation in the Communist Party agitation that led to a union strike that closed the Port of San Francisco in 1934. So it's mighty peculiar that the *New York Times*, the "newspaper of record," the paper all the other papers and all the television networks look to for direction, somehow never got around to mentioning that Harry Hay was an enthusiastic supporter of The North American Man-Boy Love Association (NAMBLA) which advocates the abolition of all age-of-consent laws. Yup, Harry was an advocate of pederasty, which Harry claimed was a natural and organic expression of male homosexuality.

The *New York Times* was not alone in this glaring omission; not a single mainstream media outlet mentioned Harry Hay's lust for boys in their obituaries and retrospectives. A Nexis database search of Harry Hay obituaries from over 30 newspapers, including the *Los Angeles Times,* the *Associated Press* and *Time* magazine, turned up not even one mention of Harry Hay's enthusiastic endorsement of NAMBLA, though all of them knew about it. This is a perfect example of how the liberal mainstream news media sanitize their news coverage of the gay social agenda.

In the eighties and nineties, as gay activists began to sanitize their public image, NAMBLA was ordered to forgo its customary appearance in the Gay Pride parades. This snub outraged Harry Hay and other up-front gays. In 1994, Harry Hay was a signer of the "Spirit of Stonewall" proclamation that argued against banning NAMBLA from the New York "pride" parade. The Spirit of Stonewall (SOS) proclamation read in part:

4

"Stonewall was a spontaneous action of marginal people oppressed by the mainstream – teenaged drag queens, pederasts, transsexuals, hustlers, and others despised by respectable straights and 'discreet' homosexuals. "SOS is an ad hoc committee of lesbian, gay and other individuals and groups formed to bring Stonewall 25 [celebrating the 25th anniversary of the riots] back to the principles of gay liberation. We focus on one of the most glaring departures from those principles: the attempt to exclude [NAMBLA].

"NAMBLA's record as a responsible gay organization is well known. NAMBLA was spawned by the gay community and has been in every major gay and lesbian march…NAMBLA's call for the abolition of age of consent is not the issue. NAMBLA is a bona fide participant in the gay and lesbian movement. NAMBLA deserves strong support in its rights of free speech and association and its member's protection from discrimination and bashing"

This amazing document clearly states that the "oppressed minority" that Harry Hay sought to "liberate" was bursting with people whose behavior and psychology were a first-class ticket to social marginalization: hustlers, drag queens, the sexually confused, the surgically refurbished, and child molesters, to name a few. It is the primal urges of this jumbled gang of oddballs, later renamed the "gay community," that motivates today's gay agenda. In its blunt assertion of the raw gay essence, the Spirit of Stonewall declaration puts the lie to every cosmetically enhanced portrait of gays that appear regularly on the pages of the *New York Times*. In its heartfelt plea to protect child molesters "from discrimination and bashing" the Stonewall declaration confirms mainstream America's well-founded skepticism of the gay agenda. NAMBLA was welcomed with open arms at all the gay pride events until the pederasts became a political liability.

When the Los Angeles Gay Pride Parade excluded NAMBLA, Harry Hay taunted the parade organizers by marching in their parade wearing a sandwich board emblazoned with the words "NAMBLA Walks With Me." This moment is included by Hay's biographer, Stuart Timmons, in his *The Trouble with Harry Hay: Founder of the Modern Gay Movement.* The book includes a photo of Harry sporting his NAMBLA sandwich board. This book was widely quoted in Hay's numerous obituaries, so the media liberals must have seen this photo, and yet every liberal news source chose to conceal the truth from the American public. That's called lying by omission.

Clearly, the mainstream media treat gay issues dishonestly. The media liberals are acting in collusion with the gay activists. Business conventions for gays in the media draw hundreds of homosexual media executives; the liberal media have been thoroughly colonized by unidentified gay activists. These secret gays have a personal stake in the gay agenda and their self-serving bias colors the way every gay issue is presented to you.

In September 1999, NBC *Today Show* co-anchor Katie Couric was the speaker at a four-day convention hosted by the Atlanta chapter of the National Lesbian and Gay Journalists Association, which attracted more than 500 journalists from across America and Canada. Also featured was Richard Kaplan, the president of CNN. According to their press release, The National Lesbian and Gay Journalists Association "works within newsrooms to foster fair and accurate coverage of lesbian and gay issues..." and "currently has 1,350 members and 23 chapters in the United States and Canada with an affiliate in Germany." In other words, homosexuals filter and spin the mainstream media's reportage of homosexual activities. You are not allowed to read or see anything that has not been laundered by a radical homosexual.

Before the aggressive push by gay activists to infiltrate mainstream American culture, The North American Man-Boy Love Association was considered by gays to be just another gay organization. Here's a quote from *The Big Gay Book: A Man's Survival Guide for the 90s Gay*, by John Preston:

"Sex between youths and adults is one of the most difficult issues in the gay movement. When does a youngster have the right and the power to make his own sexual decisions? How are laws against intergenerational sex used specifically to target gay men? What are the issues that make the romantic image of the Greek teacher and

6

his student in times of antiquity turn into something ugly and forbidden in the modern age? If you want to explore these issues, NAMBLA is the organization that will supply you with brochures, thought-provoking books and booklets." A Greek *teacher* and his student? This is delusional. Perhaps it's time for gays to stop bragging about their superior social insight.

The Big Gay Book might also have mentioned that NAMBLA stands at the ready to coach all the gay guys who work in your office and live in your neighborhood that it **is** possible for a fully grown gay guy to have hot pumpin' anal intercourse with a five-year-old boy. All that is necessary is for the gay to prep the kindergartner with a pre-sodomy enema. The helpful NAMBLA team is there to convince every gay inquirer that the little tike *craves* amorous homosexual attention.

NAMBLA continues to argue for the abolition of **all** age-of-consent laws, which has made them political poison. The upper-class lesbians and gays who seek respectability and the approval of heterosexuals are desperate to conceal the creepy aspects of gay behavior. "I have been trying to convince the NAMBLA people for years that they should argue for an age of 14 or 15, something that people could see as a little more reasonable," said William A. Percy, professor of history at the University of Massachusetts/Boston and the author of *Pederasty and Pedagogy in Archaic Greece*. "But they're a small group of inbred and fanatical ideologues. They only talk to each other. They won't listen to ideas of compromise." With all due respect to the professor, even a "compromise" age-of-consent of 15 years is repulsive to normal adults.

On the Internet aging gays post pained and rapturous poetry about their ten-year-old neighbors and ruminate about the best places to take a 13-year-old date and then swap stories about the best ways to bamboozle an unsuspecting single mother. Harry Hay, the founder of gay liberation, would want you to sympathize with these long-suffering boy lovers because they have been "marginalized" by society. Harry imagined the NAMBLA gays to be an **oppressed minority**. Could it be that Harry Hay, the founder of gay liberation, was also a delusional ideologue?

The gays were embarrassed by videotapes of the warm welcome NAMBLA received at every gay-pride event; this visual evidence was awakening Americans to the dangerous implications of embracing the gay agenda. Now that gays are seeking increased legitimacy and greater social influence, the creeps of NAMBLA are suddenly outcasts. Gay bookstores now hide the *NAMBLA Bulletin* behind the counter.

Ed Hermance, owner of Giovanni's Room in Philadelphia says he yanked the *NAMBLA Bulletin* only after his staff threatened to strike. Says gay guy Hermance: "I think it's a strange day for gay culture when we start banning something because it makes us uncomfortable. Especially when that thing is a foundation of gay literature. If we pulled all the books that had adult-youth sexual themes, we wouldn't have many novels, memoirs, or biographies left." Mr. Hermance is describing the gay counterculture, complete with its own literature and its alien world view. This is the alien world that mainstream America will be embracing if it legalizes gay marriage, gay adoption, gay culture. America does not have the luxury of accepting only those parts of the gay counterculture that it finds endearing. Gay culture is all of a piece, so it's all or nothing.

Not to be outdone, lesbian feminist Gayle Rubin tells us that "Youth Liberation has argued for some time that young people should have the right to have sex as well as not to have it, and with whom they choose. The statutory structure of the sex laws has been identified as oppressive and insulting to young people. A range of sexual activities are legally defined as molestation, regardless of the quality of the relationship or the amount of consent involved." So the lesbians want to play "Greek teacher" also. In this case, something called Youth Liberation is being used as a cover for the panting desire of lesbians to lunch on our daughters.

The *Advocate* published a two-part article by lesbian theorist Pat Califia which critiqued American age-of-consent laws and,

8

according to Ms. Califia, "spurred discussion about the sexuality of young people, intimate relationships between men and boys, and the dangerous implications of banning all erotic images of minors." She's against laws banning child pornography!

To quote this lesbian theorist, "Minors who are given the power to say 'no' to being sexually used by an abusive parent or relative are also going to assume the right to say 'yes' to other young people and adults whom they desire. You can't liberate children and adolescents without disrupting the entire hierarchy of adult power and coercion and challenging the hegemony of anti-sex fundamentalist religious values."

What a mouthful. Let's unpack this creepy lesbian vision: Lesbian theorist Pat Califia is saying that if a loving parent gives his (her) child the loving lesson that the loved child has the God-given right to say "no" to the sly sexual predations of a warped adult, then that parent has simultaneously granted that child full sexual autonomy and permission to shout "yes! yes! yes!" to the sexual advances of an adult whom the child "desires," an adult with a teddy bear perhaps, or a beautiful doll, or a video game, or candy.

According to this lesbian theorist, once the child has been given permission to say "no," the child has also been "liberated" to say "yes" and once the child is liberated in this mysterious fashion "the entire hierarchy of adult power and coercion" is disrupted. This sounds grand until you understand that "the entire hierarchy of adult power and coercion" that this lesbian theorist is railing against is really just two normal parents who are scared witless that their loved child may become the object of sexual desire of some cunning adult.

Ms. Califia is not doing the children of the world any favors by spouting this crap. It's a shame that she can't see that "the hegemony of anti-sex fundamentalist religious values" that she finds so confining is just the commonsense consensus of normal people. Adults ought to direct their expressions of sexual love toward other adults and allow the children an uninterrupted period of maturation. This lesbian's reasoning is rubbish, but she has

9

given us the gift of her invaluable insight into how homosexuals view the world. We have been warned.

If the homosexual countercultures, both gay and lesbian, are given increased legitimacy by the extension of a marriage privilege, or adoption rights or any other legitimizing accommodation, then that newfound legitimacy will be used to further the invasive **hidden** gay agenda that seeks the radical transformation of every cultural institution created to support normal heterosexual relationships and the continuance of our civilization. An aggressively expanding gay comfort zone now cramps and diminishes normal cultural values and enlarges the cultural space of an alien gay sensibility. The mainstream news media have been colonized by gay activists who spin every story and censor every image that Big Journalism presents to us. The gay comfort zone has been expanding continuously since that long-ago summer evening in 1948 when the gay communist Harry Hay sat down at his kitchen table and re-imagined the homosexual sub-culture as Karl Marx might have imagined it if Karl Marx had been a homosexual.

Before Harry Hay, no one on this planet thought of homosexuals as an "oppressed minority." Gays were odd, menacing, wayward, entertaining and rogue. But a genuine minority? No. The next chapter begins with a thought experiment. Please indulge me.

Chapter Two

Imaginary Minorities: The Anorexia Analogy

Are girls with eating disorders an oppressed minority? I ask this question because the rexies are demanding some respect.

". . . if you want sympathy for your 'disease,' you are an anorexic," declared an activist on Rexia-World. "If you want respect and admiration for your lifestyle of choice, you are a rexie . . . Anorexics die. Rexies don't. Have we understood the difference? This site is for us rexies, who are proud of our accomplishments, and the accomplishments that lie ahead. We will never die."

"Starvation is fulfilling," declared one rexie. "Colors become brighter, sounds sharper, odors so much more savory and penetrating that inhalation fills every fiber and pore of the body. The greatest enjoyment of food is actually found when never a morsel passes the lips."

This may not be *your* notion of the enjoyment of food, but it *is* the opinion of someone who speaks for many other young women. Are these young women deluded or are they a social minority with perspectives a liberal society is obligated to respect?

Join me in a thought experiment. Imagine that the rexies had the benefit of a pro-ana theorist who wrote a faster's manifesto that re-imagined anorexics as an **oppressed minority.** Now imagine that some other pro-ana theorists, who were inspired by the first pro-ana theorist, were to script a very detailed media campaign for convincing all of the rest of America that anorexics were not freakishly strange people, but "really" smart, capable and in-control gals with admirable self-discipline who were making an alternative lifestyle choice that was a private matter protected by the United States Constitution.

Next imagine that the anorexics launched an aggressive campaign to disrupt speaking appearances by members of the American Psychiatric Association. Picture the rexies shouting down the

11

psychiatrists and making a shambles of their efforts to build their careers. Suppose that this campaign was so intense that the American Psychiatric Association agreed to closed-door meetings with pro-ana militants that dragged on for years and that at the end of it all the APA had agreed to allow the rexies to distribute a mail-in ballot to every member of the APA asking them if it was time to drop anorexia nervosa from the APA's manual of disorders, all of it to be carefully worded and funded by the rexies. Suppose that only a statistically worthless 25% of the membership bothered to return their ballots and that the rexies just barely won that meaningless vote but got anorexia scrubbed as a disorder from the APA's definitive manual of disorders. And finally imagine that the rexies were lavishly funded by "thinspiration" advocates in the "never-too-thin, never-too-rich" fashion industry and that popular "Slenderella" Hollywood actresses gave moving appeals for pro-ana tolerance and an end to rexie bashing.

If all of this is more than you can imagine, then come to terms with these historical facts: this fanciful arc of an upcoming Rise of the Rexies is **exactly** the pathway to "gay acceptance" that was paved by homosexual activists. This is the true history of the Gay Power Movement: A gutless clutch of careerists at the American Psychiatric Association were bullied into dropping homosexuality from the APA's Diagnostic and Statistical Manual; they collapsed under a campaign of harassment and intimidation. The removal of homosexuality from the APA's list of disorders was a **political** act, not a medical assessment. A detailed history of the shameless capitulation of the APA awaits you in Chapter 10.

The media campaign of today's gay activists is modeled on a battle plan scripted by the queer theorists Marshall Kirk and Hunter Madsen (aka Erastes Pill). This strategic document is appropriately titled "The Overhauling of Straight America."

This gay war plan spells out in graphic detail a thoroughly dishonest smear campaign to malign all critics and to recast homosexuals in the public mind as *victims*. Liberals are suckers for the gay victim pose which cynical gays exploit with appeals for help. Here's an excerpt from "The Overhauling of Straight America":

"The first order of business is desensitization of the American public concerning gays and gay rights. To desensitize the public is to help it view homosexuality with indifference instead of with keen emotion. Ideally, we would have straights register differences in sexual preference the way they register different tastes for ice cream or sports games: she likes strawberry and I like vanilla; he follows baseball and I follow football. No big deal."

That is how Marshall Kirk and Hunter Madsen began their game plan for lulling normal humans into accepting the homosexual colonization of mainstream America. They continued:

"The way to benumb raw sensitivities about homosexuality is to have a lot of people talk a great deal about the subject in a neutral or supportive way. Open and frank talk makes the subject seem less furtive, alien, and sinful, more above-board. Constant talk builds the impression that public opinion is at least divided on the subject, and that a sizeable segment accepts or even practices homosexuality. Even rancorous debates between opponents and defenders serve the purpose of desensitization so long as 'respectable' gays are front and center to make their own pitch. The main thing is to talk about gayness until the issue becomes thoroughly tiresome. And when we say talk about homosexuality, we mean just that. In the early stages of any campaign to reach straight America, the masses should not be shocked and repelled by premature exposure to homosexual behavior itself. Instead, the imagery of sex should be downplayed and gay rights should be reduced to an abstract social question as much as possible. First let the camel get his nose in the tent – only later his unsightly derriere!"

They are describing a shamelessly cynical campaign to dupe normal Americans into allowing the sly encroachment of an alien and toxic subculture into the American mainstream. Both Kirk and Madsen are deeply hostile to traditional Christian perspectives; they exhort gays to spread moral confusion and to weaken

America's moral guardrails; they tell gays to ". . . use talk to muddy the moral waters." Gays are told to strike the victim pose:

"In any campaign to win over the public, gays must be cast as victims in need of protection so that straights will be inclined by reflex to assume the role of protector. If gays are presented, instead, as a strong and prideful tribe, they are more likely to be seen as a public menace that justifies resistance and oppression. For that reason, we must forego the temptation to strut our 'gay pride' publicly when it conflicts with the Gay Victim image. . ."

They are talking about using your own best instincts against your own best interests. Because the average American has never read any radical gay literature and has no clue that queer theory even exists, much less that there is a campaign afoot to "overhaul" every core institution about which American culture coheres, the average American is a sitting duck for Gay Power propaganda and gay propaganda is *everywhere*. It is in your newspaper; it is in your television news and dramas; it is bubbling out of every high school "gay/straight alliance" club; it trips from the lips of every elementary-school teacher mouthing "Heather Has Two Mommies."

Every gay activist agrees that the rotting underbelly of gay culture must be hidden from normal Americans at all cost; the straights, those idiot "breeders," must never catch a glimpse of what dwells in the hearts of millions of homosexuals. But don't trust me; hear it from the lips of the queer theorists who invented the gay agenda now being promoted by Barack Hussein Obama. In the words of Kirk and Madsen:

"A media campaign to promote the Gay Victim image should make use of symbols which reduce the mainstream's sense of threat, which lower its safeguard, and which enhance the plausibility of victimization. In practical terms, this means that jaunty mustachioed musclemen would keep a very low profile in gay commercials and other public presentations, while sympathetic figures of nice young people, old people, and attractive women would be featured. (It almost goes without saying that groups on

14

the farthest margin of acceptability such as NAMBLA [North American Man-Boy Love Association] must play no part at all in such a campaign: suspected child-molesters will never look like victims.)"

Of course not! If the Gay Power Movement is to get *any* traction then that randy bunch of frolicsome boy rapists who were, until recently, an unquestioned feature of every gay pride parade **must** be hidden from view! A deviant subculture energized by anal erotism, sado-masochism, fetishism, pederasty and lesbian child predation is making a pitch for mainstream acceptance, but without renouncing its deviant essence. This "change" is purely **cosmetic**.

The queer theorists and their acolytes stand condemned by the black-letter text of the Gay Movement's organizing manifesto which instructs the foot soldiers of Gay Power to lie, defame, distort, conceal, vilify, harass and menace – all in the name of "gay rights" and always while striking that phony victim pose. Here's another dose of twisted gay subterfuge from the gays who scripted the Gay Agenda:

"Straight viewers must be able to identify with gays as victims. Mr. and Mrs. Public must be given no extra excuses to say, 'They are not like us.' To this end, the persons featured in the public campaign should be decent and upright, appealing and admirable by straight standards, completely unexceptional in appearance – in a word, they should be indistinguishable from straights we would like to reach."

These masters of deception are talking about the sanitized homosexuals who pop out of your television during *Will & Grace* re-runs or *Grey's Anatomy* every Thursday evening. How long do you think it will be before there is an episode in which a gay arrives at the Seattle Grace emergency room with a gay-related injury – a bleeding rectum, a lacerated anal sphincter or an impossible-to-remove-without-surgery foreign object lodged in his lower colon? The answer is **never!** The victim of a gay gang rape? Never! This is what happens in **real** emergency rooms

15

but **never** happens on the stage sets of dramas written by homosexuals or their straight fellow travelers. There is a chasm between the reality of what you will discover on the gay-health websites and what you will every see on *Grey's Anatomy*. If the writers of *Grey's Anatomy* ever showed you the truth they would be shunned; they would be ostracized; they would *never* work again. Liberal fascism takes no prisoners. Because the truth does not promote the gay agenda, the truth must never be told in the liberal media.

When sexual encounters are always one genuine sex organ short of a full deck the term "normal sex" is meaningless. With everything even remotely related to human procreation completely off the menu, any weird sexual behavior is possible. But you won't see any of that weirdness in television dramas because the gay-friendly creators of your TV fare are slavishly following the guidelines scripted for them by Mr. Kirk and Mr. Madsen. Liberal "artists" resemble robots; they are programmed to never, ever, color outside the lines.

The squeamish straights must be shielded from reality. The creators of the gay agenda declare that:

"A media campaign that casts gays as society's victims and encourages straights to be their protectors must make it easier for those who respond to assert and explain their new protectiveness. Few straight women, and even fewer straight men, will want to defend homosexuality boldly as such. Most would rather attach their awakened protective impulse to some principle of justice or law, to some general desire for consistent and fair treatment in society. Our campaign should not demand direct support for homosexual practices, should instead take anti-discrimination as its theme."

Got that? The dimwit straight enablers of a thoroughly cynical gay agenda aren't *really* facilitating boy rapists and the trashing of marriage as a respectable institution, they are defending "some principle of justice" and a general desire for consistency. Here's more:

"At a later stage of the media campaign for gay rights – long after gay ads have become commonplace – it will be time to get tough with remaining opponents. To be blunt, they must be vilified . . . We intend to make the anti-gays look so nasty that average Americans will want to dissociate themselves from such types."

They go on to describe in detail how every opponent of gay desires must be vilified, defamed, and mischaracterized as a toothless backwater hillbilly with an idiotic crush on Jesus.

Gays at their best are odd and edgy and subversive. Their acidic outsider critiques of straight culture are worth a listen. It is, after all, the grindstone that makes the blade sharper. That said, every culture secures its future by maintaining the integrity of those shared values that bind together the people of that culture. Without shared values there is no coherence – everything falls apart. The outsider perspective has its place, but that place is somewhere at the margins.

Homosexuals are the products of **chance**; they are no more a minority deserving of special rights than are people who were born left-handed, club-footed or hunch-backed. Every life is a roll of the dice; left-handedness imposes difficulties in a world where 90% of the population is right-handed. Likewise, a homosexual disposition imposes frustrations when 99% of humanity is born heterosexual. That's life. Get used to it!

The great enterprise of American civilization should not be weakened by demands to re-define its organizing institutions to accommodate abnormal people with freakish lifestyles and freakish appetites. Candid homosexuals agree with me.

No topic has roiled the gays more than gay marriage or, to put it another way, the domestication of the gay soul. The modern Gay Movement with its sophisticated and sanitized media campaign, all of it scrupulously cleansed of transvestites, pederasts and fetishists, is the creature of a rather small clutch of educated upper-middle-class homosexuals who yearn to have their deviant tastes accepted as a new alternative normal. They want to win acceptance for a constellation of psychological and behavioral peculiarities that are the result of their personal biological developments gone astray. The honest queers aren't buying into this new white-gloved gay etiquette; they aren't ready to be corralled; they aren't ready for domestication.

If the upper-crust gays succeed in establishing a popular stereotype of domesticated gayness and if this new-to-history sanitized gayness becomes the bedrock of gay legitimacy, then any gay who strays from the new stereotype will stand doubly condemned as a depraved freak. Henceforth, the downward social pressure from straights and domesticated gays alike on the rogue homosexuals will be immense.

Chapter Three

Gays Against Gay Marriage

The "gay community" is far from unanimous in its opinion that same-sex marriage is worth pursuing. An Internet search using the search words "gays against gay marriage" instantly brought to light many articulate contrary opinions. Here is a taste from Jonathan Soroff's brief essay *Gays Against Adam and Steve*:

"It's demonstrably not the same thing as a marriage between a man and a woman. It's two guys or two girls, and no matter how much Mendelssohn and matching white outfits you dress it up in, the religious and social significance of a gay wedding ceremony simply isn't the same. We're not going to procreate as a couple (until science catches up), and while the desire to demonstrate commitment might be laudable, the religious traditions that have accommodated same-sex couples have had to do some fairly major contortions to do so . . . So the promise part is nice. Otherwise, 'gay marriage' is beside the point. And for precisely that reason, I find it cringe-worthy to watch gay couples aping the rituals of a heterosexual wedding ceremony."

In her essay *Will marriage change gay love?* Tracy Clark Flory worries about "the impact on gay relationships" of a "governmentally recognized happily ever after." With concern she asks, "Will the fairy-tale fantasy take hold in the same way it has for heterosexuals and shape romantic dynamics?" She is dismayed to hear from gays in the know that "that's *already happened.*" She bumped into Laurie Essig, a professor of sociology at Middlebury College who told her that "A generation of upper-class white lesbians and gays are already enamored by the idea of marriage."

So the campaign for same-sex marriage is really a quest for upper-crust respectability. These self-identified "good gays" are seeking to differentiate themselves from those bad gays who pride themselves "on the acceptance of more fluid romantic, sexual and familial relationships" as the author puts it. She quotes a 26-year-old gay graduate student at Yale who laments, "Ever since marriage was *the* gay issue, the diversity of types of gay relationships has narrowed."

Suddenly gay marriage was a big deal for young gays, but why? Gay observer Kelly McClure had an answer: "We can now legally, and in writing, demand that the person we love never ever leave us. EVER!! Or, you know, until they sign another legal document that says they can." She makes it sound a little like domesticating wolves. Michael Bronski, who teaches gender studies at Dartmouth College, recalls his gay male students describing how "their parents, their mothers in particular, are really happy that they can get married and they are looking forward to them finding the right guy." He says the parents are fearful their gay sons will contract AIDS. "For them, marriage is not so much a happy ending as *safety* – which is a complete fantasy of course. The parents think of same-sex marriage as a prophylactic."

It seems almost quaint, all these years later, to remember how Oprah Winfry galvanized America with frightening predictions of the coming *heterosexual* AIDS epidemic, an epidemic that never happened because the straight-folk commitment to biblically-defined monogamous pair bonding stood as a firewall against heterosexual mass extinction.

The New York Legislature's passage of the Marriage Equality Act prompted renewed discussion among gay activists about the value of pursuing a social convention that so thoroughly enshrines the straight-folk values of fidelity, exclusivity and monogamy. Once the relationships of the "good gays" are legitimized and cosseted in the protective cocoon of marriage, don't the "bad queers" in their open relationships or their polyamorous relationships or their preference for anonymous sex with strangers, seem even more deserving of disdain and marginalization?

This could be the beginning of the end of the "gay community." The unity of the homosexuals has always been a creature of convenience. Would gay males and lesbians spend ten minutes' time in one another's company if they did not have a shared political agenda? My home town is renowned for its tolerance of homosexuals but the gay male couples live in the big Colonials on the hill west of Valley Street and the lesbians live on the rise east of Valley Street; gay parties are conspicuous for their lopsided lack of gender balance.

When homosexuals have a way to become (sort of) respectable, there will be increased social pressure on **all** homosexuals to become respectable. All the laggards will look doubly deviant.

Based on the evidence, we must conclude that homosexuals are a **synthetic** minority because their minority status is merely the consequence of politics well played. There is no biological argument for elevating homosexuality to equality with heterosexuality; homosexuality is an unproductive biological backwater; it is the consequence of normal life-enhancing biological developments gone wrong. The natural world is riddled with such failures. Homosexuals are "natural" in the same sense that two-headed sheep are "natural;" no more significance than that can be given to their appearance in the world. Biological processes are vulnerable to corruption. Humans who are sexually attracted to other humans of their own gender are biological *accidents*; they are freaks of nature. No human culture that hoped to have a future would allow such a freakishly odd and biologically pointless disposition to share equal status with life-sustaining and future-ensuring heterosexuality.

Even aging heterosexual couples who are well beyond the age of procreation serve the immensely positive supporting function of role-modeling **normal** gender pair bonding. Heterosexual grandparents **reinforce** the role-modeling of their parenting children. Heterosexual grandparents complete the arc of modeling the humanity-preserving behaviors of normal heterosexuality.

The Gay Movement, by contrast, is merely a creature of politics, money, and a shameless willingness to tell normal people outrageous lies. As you have witnessed, the founding documents of the Gay Movement are proof-beyond-doubt that gay activists are shameless liars who are cynically exploiting the most noble inclinations of normal Americans to advance the selfish interests of their tiny and corrosive subculture.

Any sensible civilization would resist elevating an oddity that Nature has so thoroughly marginalized. A wise people would leave homosexuality exactly where Mother Nature herself has placed it – uselessly at the margins of normal heterosexual human culture.

Chapter Four

The Threat to True Marriage

After centuries of mischief making, homosexuals would have us believe that they have abandoned their former ways and embraced domesticity. In truth, an influential minority of homosexuals have chosen to momentarily mimic heterosexual restraint for the calculated purpose of mainstreaming homosexuality. A splinter faction of gay radicals want to fix in the minds of normal heterosexuals the false notion that homosexuality is an alternative **co-equal** of the universal mammalian standard of species-preserving heterosexuality. This notion is nonsense.

A normal heterosexual disposition is the consequence of many biological developments progressing normally. In every healthy human culture the **normal** inborn proclivities of heterosexuals are complemented and enhanced by social institutions and rituals that reinforce a species-preserving **normalcy.** No healthy culture idealizes any sort of deviancy, least of all sexual deviancy.

Homosexuality is deviant because every homosexual is the consequence of some normal biological development gone haywire or some normal human life interrupted by a ruinous sexual encounter with a predatory homosexual. If there were anything life-enhancing about homosexuality, homosexuals would amount to more than the trifling 1% of this planet's human population.

Homosexuals are not a genuine minority. Genuine minorities are distinguished by well-defined cultural or fixed and visible biological characteristics, and usually both in combination. Homosexuals, in sharp contrast, have no clearly defined culture and only a single psychological quirk in common – same-sex attraction. Many gays are the result of arrested development, of a failure to mature emotionally beyond the infantile stage of self-adoration.

23

Gays Slam the Door

Radical gay activists have rushed to slam the door in the faces of homosexuals who seek deeper insight into their deviancy. On New Year's Day of 2013, California became the first state to make it illegal to offer minors any therapy intended to change their sexual orientation, including any effort to "change behaviors or gender expressions, or to eliminate or reduce sexual or romantic attractions or feelings toward individuals of the same sex." This law restrains every "licensed professional" from offering any insight or assistance to minors and compels every minor seeking help to consult an **amateur** counselor.

This law is unprecedented. Never before had any form of talk therapy that didn't also include physical harm been banned. This law infringes on free-speech rights because talk therapy is just that – people talking through emotional issues.

New Jersey Assemblyman Tim Eustace is a proud gay Democrat. He has introduced legislation to outlaw "gay conversion therapy" by licensed practitioners. He argues that the government (politicians like him) must protect minors from gay conversion therapy in the same spirit in which government restricts potentially harmful activities, such as, underage drinking, indoor tanning and tobacco consumption. Completely lost on the assemblyman is the documented evidence that homosexual behaviors are the high-risk behaviors that fueled the AIDS epidemic and a standing venereal disease epidemic and a rampant contagion of a dozen other diseases that are virtually unknown among heterosexuals. Gay anal sex is a rejection of the most basic tenet of toilet training: Don't play with poop!

Psychology is not a hard science; its evidence is anecdotal. Psychology is a body of **opinions**; its many schools of thought are centered on imaginative paradigms of the human mind; psychology is equal parts observation and fantasy. That said, does reparative therapy work?

For people whose same-sex attractions are rooted in childhood family dynamics or in emotional trauma, the answer is yes. For those whose homosexuality is anchored in neurological abnormality, probably not. Indeed, a biological gay might feel worse after a go at therapy simply because he saw the therapy as his **last chance** for a "cure." If a gay is in despair when entering therapy, then a therapeutic failure may deepen that despair, but that is not a reflection on the therapy; it is simply the discovery that the gay's gayness is biological in origin and not the result of a damaging life experience. The only therapy for unhappy biological gays is palliative – philosophical reflection and self-acceptance.

The effort to ban attempts at reparative therapy is an effort to codify in law the notion that **all** homosexuality is rooted in immutable biology. This is a **political** proposition unsupported by evidence. These prohibitions will face constitutional challenges rooted in parents' rights, in religious rights, and in free speech rights. Thomas Healy, a constitutional law professor at Seton Hall Law School, believes that the proposed New Jersey law will be vulnerable on free speech grounds because it "really strikes at the heart of what psychiatrists do, which is talk people through issues."

Reclaiming Their Manhood

The November 1st, 2012 *New York Times* included an article titled " 'Ex-Gay' Men Fight Back Against View That Homosexuality Can't Be Changed." As this article relates:

"Ex-gay men are often closeted, fearing ridicule from gay advocates who accuse them of self-deception and, at the same time, fearing rejection by their church communities as tainted oddities. Here in California, their sense of siege grew more intense in September when Gov. Jerry Brown signed a law banning use of widely discredited sexual 'conversion therapies' for minors – an assault on their own validity, some ex-gay men feel."

And:

"Aaron Blitzer, 35, was so angered by the California ban, which will take effect on Jan.1, that he went public and became a plaintiff in a lawsuit challenging the law as unconstitutional.

"To those who call the therapy dangerous, Mr. Blitzer reverses the argument: 'If I'd known about these therapies as a teen I could have avoided a lot of depression, self-hatred and suicidal thoughts,' he said at his apartment in Los Angeles. He was tormented as a Christian teenager by his homosexual attractions, but now, after men's retreats and an online course of reparative therapy, he says he feels glimmers of attraction for women and is thinking about dating.

"I found that I couldn't just say 'I'm gay' and live that way," said Mr. Blitzer, who plans to seek a doctorate in psychology and become a therapist himself.

"Many ex-gays guard their secret but quietly meet in support groups around the country, sharing ideas on how to avoid temptations or, perhaps, broach their past with a female date. Some are trying to save heterosexual marriages. Some, like Mr. Blitzer, hope one day to marry a woman. Some choose celibacy as an improvement over what they regard as a sinful life."

It is not my belief that homosexuality, as such, is sinful. Homosexuals are problematic simply because their appetites, their proclivities, their collective transgressions and their social agenda are corrosive to the moral and emotional health of normal human beings and the institutions that normal humans have created to preserve a coherent and sane environment in which to raise children and continue the great enterprise of civilization. Gays don't have to be evil to be destructive; they only have to be **different** in ways that are socially subversive.

The only reason we are being subjected to the current gay-marriage dog-and-pony show is the yearning of some white upper-middle-class lesbians and gays for middle-class respectability. This tiny

26

percentage of American homosexuals is ashamed of the edgy, subversive, outlaw essence of unbridled homosexuality. These are the "white-picket-fence-and a 401K" gays who are scathingly mocked by authentic gay critics.

The Mouse That Roars

Homosexuals are not a legitimate minority; they are merely a self-proclaimed identity group with quirks. Homosexuals are no more an "oppressed minority" that teenage girls with eating disorders. The behaviors of both groups elicit **disapproval** from normal humans, but disapproval is **not** oppression.

According to revised U.S. Census data, pair-bonded homosexual couples amount to less than 1% of pair-bonded American couples. To put that another way, over 99% of American couples are heterosexual. The Census Bureau downgraded the number of same-sex couples living together in 2010 by thirty percent after it was discovered that Census workers had mistakenly miscalculated many heterosexual couples as same-sex. To put the American gay population in perspective, take note of the fact that there are 227,431,000 adults in America of whom only 2,270,000 are homosexuals (1%). Homosexuals congregate in urban areas to enhance their chances of meeting other homosexuals; their appearances at gay parades are overly impressive because these gatherings occur in the few places where gays are plentiful. The ranks of these public displays are deceptively swollen by gays who commute cross-country from parade to parade, by non-gay sympathizers, by pandering politicians and by voyeurs pathetically seeking a glimpse of those bare-breasted lesbians.

Here's the truth: the entire population of American gays is about a third of the population of a single American city, New York. Straights outnumber gays by about 99 to 1. That's because gays are biological or behavioral accidents; they are the consequence of normalcy gone wrong; they are an unintended residue of heterosexual procreation. To celebrate or idealize these developmental accidents is to subvert our civilization. The false impression that gays are a significant fraction the American population can be traced to the big noise that gays make, which is intentional. The blueprint for the loud gay propaganda campaign that now permeates our school curricula, our political contests, our popular entertainment and our news media was first articulated by the queer theorists Marshall Kirk and Hunter Madsen, as I have explained.

Any American who came of age after the publication of Kirk and Madsen's three manifestos has been marinated in false and cynical propaganda since kindergarten. Gay propagandists now hang their hopes on the fact that so many young people have been **groomed** by gay propaganda since childhood. But when questioned further these same youngsters display a stunning ignorance of homosexuality. It is commonplace for these kids to say that gays are twenty-five or thirty percent of the population, instead of the true 1%. How will they feel about homosexuality after the confused teenagers they knew in high school get over their confusion and identify as straight? Or when the few true gays they knew want to share a tent with their sons at Boy Scout camp?

A Darwinian Perspective

From the perspectives of either traditional religion or Darwinian determinism, homosexuality is a joke without a punch line – it falls flat. The religionists believe that the two sexes **complement** one another in a meaningful life-enhancing manner, and that the intention of the Creator is writ large in our biology. To the Darwinian atheist we are what we are because **what we are** allows us to survive as a species. In other words, our biological and cultural dimensions are the sum of our "adaptive fitness."

Because homosexuality is a **disaffection** for one's gender complement, homosexuality confers no survival benefit; to the degree to which it exists in any human society, it diminishes group cohesion. To put that another way, we survive as a species only because there are **so few** homosexuals.

Charles Darwin was perplexed by human altruism which seemed to contradict his basic thesis that natural selection should favor the

28

most selfish human behaviors. Darwin was puzzled by the question of why *anyone* would sacrifice his life for another before passing on his genetic inheritance. Here's the answer: We pass along our genes as individuals, but we survive as social beings **in groups** and groups can survive only if individuals are willing to defend the group. We are **social** beings. Our outstanding survival advantage is a consequence of our ability to form large and complex groups. We call these groups cultures.

Every culture enhances its chances of survival by defining itself with a distinctive language and distinctive rituals and distinctive myths. These myths are the shared stories about group origin and group identity; these stories bind the group together.

Religion is a repository of shared sacred myths. These myths are sacred, not in the least, because they facilitate group cohesion and survival. The sacred institution of marriage, together with its sustaining myths of masculine and feminine virtue, gender complementarity and the obligations of fatherhood and motherhood, is the cornerstone of human group cohesion and group survival.

In contradistinction to the demonstrated social benefits of religion and heterosexual marriage from both the religious and the Darwinian perspectives, we now have the clamoring of an ill-defined hodgepodge of males and females who are incapable of normal human pair bonding. They are a catch basket of genetic mutations, neurological oddities, wounded psyches and developmentally-delayed narcissists. All of them are demanding "inclusion" and "respect" and their "rights." They want the 99% of Americans who were born normal in accordance with God's life-enhancing Big Plan or maybe Darwin's life-enhancing natural selection, or both, to just ignore the demonstrated fact that homosexuality is a quirk without a future, that all erotic contact between homosexuals and normal people is toxic to the normal development of heterosexuals, that homosexuals are incapable of role-modeling the nuanced chemistry of normal pair bonding that is every child's birthright and that every gay "marriage" is a mocking parody of the central organizing institution of our civilization.

Even sterile couples and elderly heterosexual couples serve the supportive role of modeling the nuanced normal behaviors of purposeful heterosexuality. By contrast, gay relationships are curiosities and, at best, a distracting muddle. The similarities between gay and straight relationships are superficial.

Gays subvert the **institutional** purpose of marriage by cunningly distracting us with arguments about *individual* rights. But it is **group cohesion** that is the first purpose of every organizing social institution of our civilization. When individualism threatens group cohesion, individualism becomes the enemy of group survival.

Subverting Our Culture

The central organizing institution of our culture does not exist to showcase anyone's love or anyone's relationship. Marriage exists to fortify cultural norms, to facilitate cultural continuity, and to provide an anchor point for social cohesion. As a matter of common law and ancient custom the definition of marriage in Western Civilization is the union of one man and one woman. There have been pockets of exception occupied by polygamous heterosexuals, but the towering model has always been heterosexual monogamy.

Heterosexual marriage is the mainspring of a larger social clockwork that brings a measured life-enhancing consistency to the lives of generation after generation of psychologically normal human beings. Now a splinter faction of abnormal humans, and a politically-divided faction at that, is throwing sand into the gears of that clockwork.

The President of the United States, Barack Hussein Obama, who was never one to let Christian morality stand in the way of his political pandering, has thrown the prestige of his office behind the effort to create new and unusual wedlock modalities. Because gays and lesbians are something other than what our culture understands to be classical men and women, these newfangled single-sex wedlock modalities will not be marriages in any sense that classical men and women and traditional Christians and Jews understand to be a true marriage. These novel inventions, each one encapsulating the offbeat specialness of gay male and lesbian emotional chemistry, deserve their own special monikers. A gay male union might be called a gayriage and a lesbian union a lesbiage. But no union that enshrines the **total rejection** of normal heterosexual gender complementarity deserves to be called a marriage, for that complementarity is the very **definition** of marriage. Any union that lacks the essential emotional chemistry of classical marriage is merely a parody of classical marriage.

The *New York Times* gave its most-honored front-page above-the-fold position to the announcement "U.S. Asks Justices to Reject a Ban on Gay Marriage." (3/1/13) It began this way:

"The Obama administration threw its support behind a broad claim for marriage equality on Thursday, and urged the Supreme Court to rule that voters in California were not entitled to ban same-sex marriage there.

"In a forceful argument, the administration claimed that denying gay couples the right to marry violates the Constitution's equal protection clause . . ."

In truth, every American adult male and female has the right to marry. Some people choose to **not** marry, just as some people choose to **not** own a firearm. One of every five male homosexuals *will* marry a woman of his choice and one of every three lesbians *will* marry a man of her choice. But one-sex wedlock is not a marriage **by definition.** One-sex wedlock is an essentially different social modality.

Mr. Obama wants to strike down Proposition 8 which was approved by California voters in 2008 who sought to restore the traditional definition of marriage in California after that state's Supreme Court had twisted the definition of marriage to include

31

one-sex wedlock. This 2008 balloting was the same one that elected Obama president. There was an enormous black voter turnout for that election. When all those black folks entered the voting booth to cast a vote for president they were also presented with Proposition 8 which offered them an opportunity to restore the traditional Christian definition of marriage in California. Blacks voted overwhelmingly for Obama and also overwhelmingly for Proposition 8. When Prop. 8 passed, the homosexuals were furious; the Internet was ablaze with their rage; gays gave the word nigger an amazing workout. Obama has turned his back on those Christian voters because they were incapable of greasing him with the really big money.

Team Obama noted that California already permits gays to enter binding contractual domestic partnerships that are very much like marriages in their legal frameworks and added that "the designation of marriage, however, confers a special validation of the relationship between two individuals and conveys a message to society that domestic partnerships or civil unions cannot match."

Indeed it does, but the bigger question is why any culture that had a care for its future would choose to idealize anything as quirky and biologically pointless as same-sex attraction? This weird idea is only being considered now because America is showing the symptoms of late-stage decadence and decline.

The reference to domestic partnerships by the Obama team was a poorly-veiled threat to the people of the seven states who legalized domestic partnership. Their thanks for accommodating homosexuals was a kick in the teeth and the imposition of a novelty called "gay marriage" when, on June 26,2013, the Supreme Court let stand a district court's decision that was itself a gift to his fellow gays from the self-proclaimed homosexual judge, Vaughn Walker. The Court did not find the arguments against gay marriage to be lacking; the Court simply ruled that the plaintiffs did not have the legal standing to bring their case to court and let Walker's decision be the deciding one. Attorney General Eric Holder issued a statement that falsely conflated the gay wedlock issue with past civil rights struggles. This is what the queer theorists Kirk & Madsen called muddying the moral waters. The comparison is false because black people are the result of **normal** biological development while homosexuals are the result of **abnormal** development. Homosexual psychology is **abnormal** psychology.

All attempts to liken Proposition 8 to the 1967 case of *Loving v. Virginia* in which the Supreme Court struck down a ban on interracial marriage are false and misleading. The few state laws that banned interracial marriage back then were of recent origin. Interracial marriage had been commonplace throughout America before these few laws were enacted; these laws were pretty much a localized phenomenon with no deep historical roots. Heterosexual marriage, by contrast, is ancient and deeply anchored in human biology. In every human culture heterosexual marriage has emerged as an expression of healthy human nature.

To elevate a **parody** of time-honored marriage to co-equal status with marriage for the sole purpose of gratifying the emotional needs of a few behavioral outliers is to mock the serious purpose for which marriage was instituted. We can be forgiven for suspecting that if one of every six of Obama's big-bucks bundlers had **not** been a homosexual before the last election, Eric Holder would not now be carrying water for the homosexual agenda.

The Obama/Holder legal brief disparaged Proposition 8's defense of ancient norms as an "impermissible prejudice," but Californians weren't *pre-judging* anything. The evidence was apparent: the time-honored institution of Judeo-Christian marriage is available to every adult not already married; everyone is free to choose marriage or leave it alone. Traditional marriage is the wellspring of Western Civilization and it is in no need of mocking parodies. Let's face it, having a quasi-autistic lack of attachment to persons of your complementary gender is a disability. The "gay community" is **self-marginalized** for no other reason than its abnormal appetites.

Barack Obama misled America: "[I]f we are truly created equal, then surely the love we commit to one another must be equal, as

33

well," he intoned in his Second Inaugural Address. But the struggle to defend traditional marriage is not about the quality or the amount of anyone's love; it's about the preservation of a vital and intact social institution.

If the **gender** aspect of the traditional definition of marriage is suddenly deemed arbitrary and based on "impermissible prejudice" then so is the **number** aspect of that definition. There are court cases pending that seek the decriminalization of heterosexual polygamy and the plaintiffs in those cases are keeping a close watch on all of the gay-marriage cases. Gay marriage is now a stalking horse for the polygamists and a Trojan Horse for the rest of us.

Making the institution of marriage all-inclusive blurs the definition of marriage beyond recognition and obliterates its culture-preserving purpose. Keeping the institution of monogamous heterosexual marriage intact should be a critical governmental objective. But instead of preserving a central organizing institution of our culture, Barack Obama is shamelessly pandering to his homosexual bundlers and bagmen.

Chapter Five

Gay Liars and Liberal Idiots

The most destructive ideologies of modern times have favored the notion that an essential human nature does not exist or, at most, is faint and extremely elastic. The enemies of civilization **must** subvert the idea that humans cannot be conditioned to accept **any** behavior, no matter how grotesque. These practitioners of human desensitization understand that getting humans to accept a repugnant behavior requires a slow and persistent exposure to behaviors that were previously felt to be disgusting. The enemies of civilization believe that humans **as humans** share no guiding moral sensibility. "Little by little we were taught all these things. We grew into them," recalled the socialist mass murderer Adolph Eichmann.

Every modern permutation of authoritarianism, socialism pre-eminent among them, has promoted the idea that humans are born as moral "blank slates" awaiting socialization. These radical egalitarians turn a blind eye to any evidence of an innate human nature because an innate human nature threatens their quest for *absolute* equality, which they hold to be the hallmark of social progress. It's an article of *faith* for them; it's a *religious* precept.

They are wrong. Our inborn human dispositions *anticipate* a range of real-world experiences; our inborn traits are activated by environmental stimuli. The environment calls forth the flowering of our *innate* abilities; the environment resonates with a human neurology already highly structured and disposed to specialized development. Temperament and sex differences are mostly genetic and fixed. Our language facility, our number sense, our tool-using facility and our moral sense are inborn. It is our moral sense that passes judgment on our natural inclinations to violence, lying, cheating and clannishness; this moral sensibility is a powerful shaping influence in every culture. Human altruism has a survival benefit for social humans but we are not born virtuous (noble savages); we are born social and redeemable; we struggle to realize our better selves in the face of many seductive distractions.

Every healthy culture, every culture that is not in an end-stage downward death spiral of moral confusion and decadence accommodates and idealizes only the most healthful inborn inclinations of its normal members; it marginalizes the dead-end behaviors of those few who are inclined toward useless or destructive deviance. The future of any culture is assured by the fulsome accommodation of that culture's **normal** members. Accommodating upstart subcultures that are hostile to the values of the core culture is a self-destructive behavior that no robust culture would exhibit. The accommodation of homosexuality and homosexual counter-cultural perspectives by President Barack Obama and his political party is evidence that America is circling the drain pipe. When the president of the United States of America declares that sterile one-sex wedlock *must* be elevated to co-equal status with time-honored, fertile, and society-sustaining heterosexual marriage, the stink of decadence is in the air. One of every six of Mr. Obama's big-bucks bundlers is a homosexual; homosexuals are *sixteen times* more abundant among Mr. Obama's financiers than in the general population; Mr. Obama was beholding to homosexuals for his continued hold on the presidency; Mr. Obama is bought and paid for by the homosexual radicals.

Brainwashing the Idiots

The founding queer theorists of the Gay Power Movement were masters of scientific persuasion. Marshall Kirk graduated *magna cum laude* from Harvard University, majoring in psychology; he went on to become a researcher in neuropsychiatry, a branch of medicine that studies mental disorders attributable to diseases of the nervous system. Erastes Pill was the chosen pen name of Dr. Hunter Madsen, who held a PhD in politics from Harvard and went on to become an expert in public persuasion, social marketing and Madison Avenue salesmanship. He chose the name Erastes because it shares the same root word as *pederasty* – man-boy sexual relations or, what normal people call boy rape.

These two enthusiasts weren't amateurs; they were educated experts who used **science** as a weapon against the life-sustaining instincts of the average American; these two deviates used their insights to undermine the central organizing institution of American society: heterosexual marriage.

In their three collaborative works, *The Gay Agenda* (1985), *The Overhauling of Straight America* (1987) and *After the Ball: How America Will Conquer Its Fear and Hatred of Gays in the 90s* (1989), they exhorted homosexuals to conceal their weirdness and to lie shamelessly to straights about every disquieting aspect of homosexuality. Here's a snippet from *The Overhauling of Straight America* by the two genius manipulators, Marshall Kirk and Hunter Madsen (Erastes Pill):

"Where we talk is important. The visual media, film and television, are plainly the most powerful image-makers in Western civilization. The average American household watches over seven hours of TV daily. Those hours open up a gateway into the private world of straights, through which a Trojan Horse might be passed. As far as desensitization is concerned, the medium is the message – of normalcy. So far, gay Hollywood has provided our best covert weapon in the battle to desensitize the mainstream. Bit by bit over the past ten years, gay characters and gay themes have been introduced into TV programs and films (though often this has been done to achieve comedic and ridiculous affects). On the whole the impact has been encouraging. The prime-time presentation of Consenting Adults on a major network in 1985 is but one high-water mark in favorable media exposure of gay issues. But this should be just the beginning of a major publicity blitz by gay America."

And that's what happened. Since 1985 your television has been a Trojan Horse bursting with subversive messages scripted by homosexuals to undermine the hard-won wisdom of normal Christians, Jews, Muslims, and just plain normal heterosexual people. The persistent repetitive gradualism advocated by these gay theorists is an echo of Eichmann's "little by little." It is cynically intended to erode our once-healthy culture's firewall against biologically pointless and morally confusing homosexuality. The sly grooming of straight Americans to accept homosexual perspectives has been a pet project of America's liberal news and entertainment media for twenty-five years; America's children have been the targets of this campaign of values reprogramming for all of their lives.

It is worth remembering that *every* television drama that features a gay character **wildly** exaggerates the number of gays in America. For example, in order to put the lesbian couple in the popular television series *Grey's Anatomy* in its proper perspective, every episode that included the lesbian couple would also have to include **almost two hundred** named and regularly-featured **heterosexual** cast members. If gays were as common as they appear in the media, the human species would be nearing extinction. Homosexuals are the consequence of normal human development gone wrong; that's why they number only about 1% of the population.

Chapter Six

Why Gays Fail the Minority Standard

Homosexuals place great emphasis on a sketchy body of evidence to proclaim that **all** homosexuality is rooted in biology. They do this for **political** reasons. First of all, they know that many straights will make the mistake of confusing the notion of "natural" with the concepts of "good" and "moral," which is nonsense. Second, homosexual activists want homosexuals to qualify as a "minority" under the narrow provisions of the 1964 Civil Rights Act. To qualify as a protected class homosexuals must demonstrate that, as a group, they share a history of discrimination and are powerless to escape their category and were **born that way.**

Right away the gay advocates have problems. The evidence does not support firm answers to these three questions. Some unknown percentage of homosexuals are the consequence of quirky biology but all we can say with certainty is that most gays are the products of some normal biological progression gone haywire. No doubt many gays were brought to homosexuality by some life experience. There is a lively literature by some very smart homosexuals who argue persuasively that they are homosexuals **by choice**. These gays give the biological-determinists nightmares because homosexuals **choosing** to be homosexual disqualifies gays **as a group** from consideration as a protected minority under the 1964 Civil Rights Act. Oops!

Dr. Lillian Faderman, winner of the Lambda Literary Foundation's Monette/Horowitz Award, says candidly that homosexuals "continue to demand Rights, ignoring the fact that human sexuality is fluid and flexible, acting as though we are stuck in our category forever." She explains that, "The narrow categories of identity politics are obviously deceptive." She senses the threat that the truth poses to gay political objectives when she reveals that, "I must confess that I am both elated and terrified by the possibilities of a bisexual movement. I'm elated because I truly believe that bisexuality is the natural human condition. But I'm much less happy when I think of the possibility of huge numbers of bisexuals (two-thirds of women who identify as lesbian for example) running off to explore the heterosexual side of their bisexual potential and, as a result, decimating our political ranks."

Got that? Dr. Faderman is "terrified" at the thought of two-thirds of America's lesbians **choosing** to ditch their lesbian partners and trotting off to explore their "heterosexual side."

Dr. Faderman is a fountain of insight when she declares that, "The concept of gay and lesbian identity may be nothing but a social construct, but it has been crucial, enabling us to demand the rights that are due to us as a minority. What becomes of our political movement if we openly acknowledge that sexuality is flexible and fluid, that gay and lesbian does not signify 'a people' but rather a 'sometime behavior'?"

Amazing! An eminent award-winning gay expert on gayness is confessing that homosexuals are not a genuine minority in **any** sense. The brilliant doctor is telling us that gays are not a biological minority like black people because gays **choose** to be gay; gays can escape their category at will. This ability to escape disqualifies homosexuals from consideration as a true minority under the provisions the 1964 Civil Rights Act.

This is nothing less than an admission that radical gays are cynically employing the Big Lie propaganda technique of made infamous by the Third Reich. To be successful, the Hitler had declared, your lie must be an enormous lie. There is no bigger lie infiltrating America than the lie that homosexuals are an oppressed minority.

Next we have Dr. John DeCecco, a psychologist and Director of the Center for Research and Education in Sexuality at San Francisco State University and editor of *The Journal of Homosexuality.* The doctor self-identifies as "gay" but insists that sexual attraction is a preference, not a fixed orientation. In his book *If You Seduce a Straight Person You Can Make Them Gay* Dr. DeCecco blows off the whole "born gay" idea as just so much "gay and lesbian politics" deployed to win social acceptance.

40

Now consider the telling insights of Dr. Vera Whisman, author of *Queer by Choice: Lesbians, Gay Men, and the Politics of Identity*, who tells us that "The political dangers of a choice discourse go beyond the simple (if controversial) notion that some people genuinely choose their homosexuality. Indeed, my conclusions question some of the fundamental basis upon which the gay and lesbian rights movement has been built. If we cannot make political claims based on an essential and shared nature, are we not left once again as individual deviants? Without an essentialist [born gay] foundation, do we have a viable politics?"

What a question. Of course not! The gay, transvestite, lesbian, transsexual, bi-sexual and "questioning" coalition has never been anything but a patched-together hodgepodge of needy oddballs in search of companionship.

Did any of the lawyers who have fumbled every courtroom defense of traditional marriage ever think to quote lesbian writer Jennie Ruby who candidly admits, "I don't think lesbians are born . . . I think they are made . . . The gay rights movement has (for many good and practical reasons) adopted largely an identity politics."

Likewise, lesbian author Jan Clausen declares, "What's got to stop is the rigging of history to make the either/or look permanent and universal. I understand why this argument may sound exotic to outsiders for whom the public assertion of a coherent, unchanging lesbian or gay identity has proved an indispensable tactic in the battle against homophobic persecution."

She's talking about the straight enablers of the gay political agenda who are too stupid to grasp the fact that they are the dupes and flunkeys of the gay Big Lie – the lie that *every* homosexual is the product of immutable biological determinism. Why should straights believe this political talking point if gays themselves don't believe it? The entire Gay Power movement is tainted with bad faith. As the lesbian poet Audre Lorde opined, "I don't believe our wants have made all our lies holy."

41

If homosexuals are queer by choice, then why would any sane civilization weaken the integrity of its central organizing institution, marriage, just to accommodate a tiny splinter population who are willfully sexually deviant?

Can we believe the lesbians Lyne Harne and Elaine Miller when they tell us that, "There's nothing natural in lesbianism, it's a 'positive choice' and a political one"? The totally gay *Girlfriends* magazine opines, "No wonder lesbians are so nervous. What makes the lesbian movement strong is the formation of a collective identity, unified behind sexual orientation as a category. If bisexuality undoes that, it kicks the lesbian movement where it really hurts: in the heart and soul of identity politics."

In other words, lots of so-called "lesbians" are just slumming in the "gay community" until its time for them to get serious about their futures and settle down with Mr. Right. They are telling us that the ranks of the "gay community" are swollen with people who will indulge in homosexual activity and then choose to leave it alone.

Kate Kendall, the Director of the National Center for Lesbian Rights challenged the American Psychiatric Association to stop offering any form of reparative therapy to any homosexual, no matter how desperately the gay begged for it. She insisted that homosexuality was inborn and immutable. She and her sidekick, Joanne Loulan, told the APA that offering reparative therapy to a homosexual was the moral equivalent of pouring bleach on a black person's skin to make them white.

Kendal would later argue in a gay publication that human sexuality is **changeable**. Ms. Loulan later drew the attention of the gay magazine *The Advocate* (2/18/97) by declaring that she had changed her own sexual orientation and had fallen deeply in love with *a man*. Oh, the horror!

What Have We Learned?

From the scientific, historical and anecdotal evidence we can conclude several things. First among them is the demonstrated willingness of gay activists to shamelessly tell any lie that will advance the Gay Power agenda. The founding mentors of the Gay Power movement, Marshall Kirk and Hunter Madsen, stressed the importance of concealing the true nature of homosexual thought and behavior from all those useful straight idiots. Second, the evidence that homosexuality is immutably rooted in biology is confusing at best. There are many paths to homosexuality; some are biological while others are experiential or some combination of biology and experience. The gay movement is bursting with lots of confused people who don't know what they are. By any accounting, homosexuals are a muddle. Their spokesmen publicly insist that *every* gay was born that way, but privately bemoan the fact that millions of "gays" flutter away from the "gay community" to mate with heterosexuals.

The best-educated gay psychologists in America are presenting articles in gay publications that negate any rightful claim by homosexuals to be a biologically-based minority "just like black people." None of the racial characteristics that distinguish black people are the consequence of some biological process **gone haywire.** Black people are **not** the result of a failure to develop normally. Black people are normal; homosexuals are abnormal. Every homosexual is the consequence of some life-enhancing process **interrupted.**

The "gay community" is really a catch basin of randomly damaged human beings, not a healthy self-sustaining community of biologically complementary humans like the 99% of humanity who are naturally-occurring heterosexuals. Without a continual influx of damaged humans, the "gay community" would wither away to extinction.

Only a small fraction of the American population who are homosexual is waging the political, judicial and propaganda campaigns that are warping American culture. These few oddballs are nonetheless a needy gaggle of sophisticated and well-heeled upper-middle-class white lesbians and gays who know how to manipulate the emotions of foolishly well-intentioned voters and enlist the aid of clueless enablers in the mass media – the fools whom the leftists cynically call "the useful idiots."

As you have seen, even the most educated and ardent advocates for homosexuality as a "true minority" are privately doubtful. Away from the courtroom and the television cameras, homosexual intellectuals candidly admit that homosexuality is a fluid and ill-defined disposition that is often a disposition **of choice**. Many gays believe their sexual orientation to be an aesthetic or a political **choice**. Homosexuals with doctorate degrees are fretting that millions of self-identified homosexuals might one day **choose** to identify as straight and leave the gay political agenda in the lurch.

These are the voices of politically astute homosexuals demonstrating their disrespect for normal heterosexual Americans. These gays insist that **you** can't be told the truth because **you** would be shocked and disgusted by the truth. For this reason, **you** must be misled like every other useful idiot of progressive socialist lore. **You** must be hoodwinked at every turn. **You** must be gulled into believing that your ruinous capitulation to the Gay Power agenda is *really* just an act of compassion.

Chapter Seven

Homophobia

The groundwork of the modern quest for gay acceptance was laid decades before by such avatars of "sexual liberation" as Margaret Mead and Alfred Kinsey, both of whom produced persuasive volumes of pseudo-science that would cause America to question its moral foundations.

Mead's book *Coming of Age in Samoa* purported to be a truthful account of the sexual and social habits of the Samoans. Mead relied on interviews with a handful of Samoan girls. Mead knew only as much of the Samoan language as she could pick up in one quick course. The girls, who were practicing Christians, were a bit taken aback by the young anthropologist's prurient interest in every detail of Samoan sexual behavior.

To please Miss Mead, the girls began to feed her fanciful stories of carefree Samoan sexual high jinks, including stories of easy-going guilt-free homosexuality. The young and gullible Margaret Mead swallowed these silly tall tales whole. *Coming of Age in Samoa* hit the bookstores like a bombshell in 1928, and it caused many Americans to question their own moral restraints. It was completely bogus, but it sounded progressive and it came wrapped in the mantel of *science*. In later years Margaret Mead would say: "I have spent most of my life studying the lives of other peoples – far away peoples – so that Americans might better understand themselves." In fact, Mead's pseudo-science only made good people question themselves for no good reason. Her suggestion that human behavior was infinitely elastic and that homosexuality was common and accepted among the Samoans was false, but widely believed.

While Mead's work was that of an ignoramus, Alfred Kinsey's work was that of an immoral pervert and felon. Kinsey was a zoologist-turned-sex-pioneer. Before he turned to human sexual studies he was best known as the world's foremost authority on the gall wasp.

Kinsey's *Sexual Behavior in the Human Male* hit the American consciousness in 1948, exactly two decades after *Coming of Age in Samoa*. The world had recently been turned upside down by a calamitous war and was struggling to reestablish traditional social habits of living. Kinsey's book complicated that effort. The 800-page book sold about half a million copies at $6.50. How many people actually endured its dry scientific prose is in question. Most Americans received "highlights" of the Kinsey Report from progressive intellectuals and media personalities. America was told over and over again that a "scientific study" had determined that ten percent, or more, of American men were essentially homosexual in nature. Overnight Alfred Kinsey became a shining apostle of the emerging Sexual Revolution. Kinsey's report inspired Harry Hay to form the Mattachine Society, which argued that homosexuals were ten percent of the population and were therefore an oppressed minority class.

Is it true that homosexuals are at least ten percent of the American population? Are they a minority that rivals in majesty our African-American population? The answer is "No." Kinsey's statistics are junk science at its worst. They are also evidence of breathtaking criminality.

When Judith Reisman plodded through Kinsey's 800-page *Sexual Behavior in the Human Male* she began to ask herself the kind of troublesome questions that people with scruples have a habit of asking. How, for example, did Alfred Kinsey "know" that an eleven month old child was capable of ten sexual orgasms in one hour? How did he know that a two-year-old could have eleven orgasms in sixty-five minutes, or a twelve-year-old could experience three orgasms in three minutes? Can a thirteen-year-old child really have twenty-six orgasms in one day? How could Alfred Kinsey discover such things?

After some determined investigation, Judith Reisman (PhD) discovered that Doctor Kinsey had collaborated with homosexual child molesters who gave him access to their sexual predation diaries. Much of the data seems to have come from a single old pederast. Kinsey aided and abetted this felonious behavior. Need it be said that having sex with your scientific subjects is not science; it's just a romp. Collegial collusion and a code of silence among professionals of like mind completed the deception. Almost two hundred children were victimized by Alfred Kinsey's illegal "research."

When Judith Reisman blew the whistle on the Kinsey data the Kinsey Institute published an 87-page packet for use by the progressive media just in case they should interview her. One of these packets landed on the desk of Dr. Paul Gebhard, the former head of the Kinsey Institute. Dr. Gebhard wrote back to the Kinsey Institute:

"In your recent letter of December 3, which I gather was sent to a number of individuals as well as me, you refuted Judith Reisman's allegations about Kinsey and the Institute. However, I fear that your final paragraph on page 1 may embarrass you and the university if it comes to Reisman's attention. Hence I want to warn you and the relevant university officials so that some damage control might be devised. The paragraph ends with this sentence: 'He *never* used data from the special samples, derived from such populations as the gay community or prisons, to generalize to the general public.' This statement is incorrect. Kinsey did mix male prison inmates with his sample used in *Sexual Behavior in the Human Male*."

Dr. Gebhard is referring to the fact that 26% of Kinsey's white male subjects were known sex offenders. An additional 25% of the subject population were convicts in prison. Some were "pimps," "thieves," and "hold-up men"; about 4% were male prostitutes. Many were habitual patrons of gay bars. It was this collection of convicts, outcasts and deviates that Kinsey blended into his data and fobbed off on America as a representative sample of American manhood. Kinsey's data are junk. Alfred Kinsey, the father of the Gay Revolution, was a fake and worse. Recent surveys have pegged the gay population at less than 3%.

In the three decades since the 1969 Stonewall Riot homosexuality has gone from what Oscar Wilde coyly called "the love that dare

47

not speak its name" to being the love that can't stop blabbering about itself. In 1999 that lovable rascal Bill Clinton declared the month of June, the traditional month of weddings, to be Gay and Lesbian Pride Month. It was a White House first. The National Park Service has added the Stonewall Inn to the National Register of Historic Places, beside Gettysburg and Appomattox Courthouse. After decades of agitation and argument the question still remains: will the larger population ever accept homosexuals without reservation? Will the larger population ever be completely comfortable with homosexuality?

Perhaps Harvey Fierstein can point us in the right direction. Mr. Fierstein expressed his anger at what he took to be the hypocrisy of sympathetic straight people: "They'll shake your hand, they'll march with us, they'll go for gay civil rights, they'll talk about housing and employment, and all that, but *don't have sex.* Don't put that thing in your mouth. *Please* don't put that thing in your mouth." It was the perfect insight. Most straight people are uncomfortable with the particulars of gay sex acts. What are the roots of this squeamishness?

Squeamishness itself is a mild form of disgust. Like its cousins, anger and shame, disgust plays a key role in the moral life of humans. Disgust is not innate, it is a *learned* emotion and it is an expression of our essential humanity. Dogs and young children are perfectly happy playing with, and even eating, their own excrement. It is only adults *who have been taught* to be horrified by such behavior, who are horrified by it.

Indeed, our first lessons in disgust begin with toilet training. Feces are the universal disgust substance. Children must be taught that poop is yucky. Later, this fussy judgmental emotion will be directed toward other squishy, crawly, slimy, smelly things. As the child matures, this most moral of emotions will be used to take the measure of less material things such as behaviors, images or abstract ideas. Soon our disgust responses become second nature, a part of our essence. Eventually, we learn to be offended by the history of things; the idea of contamination, both actual and spiritual, becomes a dimension of our disgust response.

48

A favorite test item used by disgust researchers Paul Rozin and Jonathan Haidt (University of Pennsylvania) is Hitler's sweater. People were asked if they would wear Hitler's sweater. The answer?

"No."

"What if we washed it?"

"No."

"What if we completely unraveled it and then knitted a new sweater from the yarn?"

"Still no."

The sweater had become unalterably spiritually contaminated. Said psychologist Rozin: "You can't do anything for most people to make it un-Hitlered."

To repeat, the seat of all this judgment making is the potty seat. It all begins with toilet training. Now consider: the most emotionally charged homoerotic image is that of a male human plunging his erect penis into another male's anal sphincter and deep into his rectum. This is the image that makes straight people really squirm because it's a direct contradiction of the excrement taboo. The participants have stained themselves with the universal disgust substance; they have become spiritually contaminated. This explains why male homosexuals are so often the targets of strong emotion while lesbians are regarded as little more than curiosities. Most people find the casual violation of our earliest taboo simply disgusting.

This is discouraging news for gays who desire social acceptance because it means that the gay agenda must buck the American Way of Toilet Training, which is, well . . . downright American and not likely to change any time soon.

Further complicating the effort for gay social acceptance is the AIDS epidemic. Any disease is perceived as a contamination. That this disease is fatal, sexually transmitted and largely confined to one identifiable deviant community makes it seem especially hellish, a revolting conflation of viral and spiritual contamination. To those people who are disposed toward harsh judgments it seemed that a terrible judgment had been passed on gay Americans. People feared contagion. At one time the life expectancy of the average American homosexual male had shrunk to only 43 years of age. Then, as if to prove that there isn't any public relations nightmare that can't be made even worse with enough effort, Gay America coined a word to throw at anyone who didn't see things their way: homophobia.

This word had remained quietly between the covers of psychology texts for decades. In psych circles it was defined as that anxiety experienced by people with unacknowledged homoerotic proclivities at those moments when their repressed homoerotic feelings unexpectedly well up and threaten to burst upon their consciousness. It's a kind of panic attack triggered by homoerotic feelings, the way arachnophobia is a panic attack triggered by an unexpected encounter with spiders. When gays say they are against homophobia they do not have this definition in mind. That would be like saying you were against claustrophobia.

In our current political discourse the word homophobia is just a brick to throw at someone's head. The person who uses it intends to imply that his opponent is afflicted with some vague sort of psychological problem or moral failing. Straight people, it suggests, have a *problem* with perfectly nice homosexuals; these straights should seek immediate remedial counseling.

Observation suggests that any true fear of homosexuals by heterosexuals is pretty much confined to parental concerns about child molestation, child seduction and child moral corruption. Gay activists insist that such concerns are silly, wrongheaded and rooted in malicious stereotypical notions about their altogether nice gay community. What is the truth?

A review of gay literature reveals that gay activists have done something clever: they have simply *defined* themselves in such a way as to avoid criminal accusations. The word "homosexual" has been redefined to mean someone who shares erotic experiences with other adults. Any male who has sexual contact with someone below the age of consent must now be called a *pedophile*. Adults who have sex with children are said to have regressed to some earlier stage of psychological development and must not be identified as homosexuals because all true homosexuals are mature people who only have sex with adults. According to this new politically-correct definition it is *impossible* for any homosexual to be a child molester because the instant he molests a child he ceases to be a homosexual and miraculously becomes a pedophile. It's the miracle of new-age propaganda and it is pure rubbish. Gays are saying that most homosexual molestation is not done by homosexuals! What every normal person means by the word homosexual is any human being who initiates sex with, or forces his sexual attentions upon, someone of his own sex, regardless of the age of the other person. That's the schoolyard definition most people use. Common sense tells us that *some* homosexual men have sex with boys. A responsible parent would want to know if the *real* threat to their child warranted any heightened defensiveness. In any case, the defining line for pedophilia is not the legal age of consent – it is puberty.

The Gay Molester Density

These are the facts: to the best of our knowledge 96% of all sexual predators are male. Boys are 22% of sex-crime victims. Gay men are, at most, about 3% of our population. From these three facts we may conclude that 97% of our population (straight men) cause 78% of the molestations (girl victims), while 3% of our population (gay men) cause 22% of molestations (boy victims). We might now invent something called the Molester Density by which to compare the gay and straight communities. The Molester Density for the straight community would be the ratio of its percentage of child molestations (78) to its percentage of the population (97), which is 78 divided by 97 which equals 0.804. The Molester Density for the gay community is the percentage of its molestations (22) divided by its percentage of the population (3), which equals 7.333.

In other words, the gay community is responsible for at least 9.12 times as many child molestations for every one percent of its population than is the straight community, which raises a big warning flag for worried parents. More realistic estimates put the number of homosexual males at 1% of the population, which increases the Molester Density of gays to **28 times** that of heterosexual males. The sly attempt by the gay community to convince you that men who molest boys are either stuck at some early stage of sexual development or have regressed to some early stage of sexual development, obscures the fact that according to classical psychoanalytical thinking homosexuals themselves are thought to be people whose arrested sexual development has left them fixated on their own gender. This sly attempt at self-sanitization raises a big red flag because it is an attempt to fool us. Remember: the defining line for pedophilia is *puberty;* it is not the age of consent. The clergy scandal that engulfed the Catholic Church was mostly about adult males forcing themselves upon post-pubescent teenagers. These creeps weren't pedophiles; they were ordinary gay males.

Don't expect to get a clear picture of the gay community from the mainstream media either. A survey of reporters by the American Society of Newspaper Editors revealed that sixty-five percent of them describe themselves as Democrat/liberal. Another survey revealed that almost ninety percent of editors described themselves as liberal. In other words, America's newspapers are top-heavy with the very sort of people who for decades have encouraged the loosening of restraints on all sorts of sexual behavior. Do these liberals censor and shade the news? Two examples will give you some idea.

Example One: On September 25, 1999 a couple of gay lovers, Josh Brown (22) and Davis Carpenter (38), got a hankering for some hot pumpin' gay sex, so they grabbed a seventh-grader, bound his wrists, and dragged him into their love nest. The gay lovers stuffed the boy's underwear into his mouth and secured it in place with a bandana and duct tape. They used belts to bind his legs and ankles together. The boy's wrists were secured to opposite sides of a mattress. The boy was positioned face down and then pillows were placed under his stomach to raise his buttocks higher. Then the homosexual attack on the boy's anus began.

Brown raped the boy repeatedly with his penis, a cucumber, a sausage, a banana and a douche bottle. Brown injected an enema into his helpless victim made from Brown's own urine. Brown rammed a cucumber part way into the boy's anus and held it there with duct tape. While all this was going on Brown's lover, Davis Carpenter, stood by, leering and masturbating wildly.

When they grew tired, the gay rapists left their bound victim and went to the kitchen for sandwiches. They didn't think that they were doing anything strange. The sadistic bondage of boyish victims is a staple of the multi-billion-dollar gay pornography industry. Things went south for these thrill-happy gays when they returned to the bedroom and discovered that their thirteen-year-old sex slave was not breathing. Jesse Dirkhising was dead.

At trial Brown used the "my daddy made me do it" defense. He called Carpenter a "domineering roommate" and insisted that the older man had directed the gay rapefest. While the dead boy's mother sat weeping and clutching a teddy bear and a photograph of her son, Brown's disgusting lawyer tried to convince the jury that the dead boy had been having consensual sex with Brown when he died. He suggested that the dead youngster and his killer were really good friends. If they were such good friends, Prosecutor Bob Balfe wondered aloud, why was the dead boy drugged with amitryptiline, a powerful sedative that hastened his death? Why was it necessary to make a late-night run for more duct tape: was the boy struggling? Why did they leave the boy bound and gagged? Why did they only pick up two sandwiches, instead of three? In truth, Brown and Carpenter were sadistic gay rapists who had killed a child, something even the Marquis de Sade never managed to do.

So how did America's liberal media report this lurid case of two homosexuals who savagely raped and killed a child? Well, the *New York Times*, which had published 195 stories about the murder of Matthew Shepard, suppressed the story entirely. The Associated Press, which had splashed the Shepard murder all over America, chose to withhold the Dirkhising murder from the national wire. The Associated Press released the story to a couple of local markets near the crime scene but was careful not to describe the killers as homosexuals. This is the same AP that ran the headline *"Openly gay student critically injured in Wyoming attack"* the day after Matthew Shepard was beaten by two goons he had hooked up with in a bar. A day later the AP ran a 700-word story with the headline *"Gay student clings to life after savage beating."* The next day brought the headline *"Call for tougher laws after attack on gay student."* The Shepard murder was reported as a national story every day for a week after Shepard's death by the Associated Press. By contrast, the liberal *Washington Post* published only one short Associated Press story about the hideous Dirkhising slaying. There was complete silence on the Dirkhising case from NBC Nightly News, Dateline NBC, CNN news, and, of course, The Today Show. Both Bill Clinton and his lesbian Attorney General Janet Reno had been very vocal about the Shepard slaying, but both of them fell silent in the face of the grotesque Dirkhising murder, even though the crime took place in Clinton's home state of Arkansas.

The networks made lame excuses about having too much other news to cover every day; they dismissed this lurid story as "local news." Since when do the media shun lurid child slayings? A three-word reminder: Jon Benet Ramsey.

So why is it that you are not allowed to witness evidence of brutal acts committed by gays? The principal reason is that America's newsrooms have become bastions of gay privilege. The media eagerly seek out affirmative-action homosexuals. Almost all of the national media outlets have recruiting booths at the National Gay and Lesbian Journalists Association convention every year. The media help to bankroll these conventions by placing up-beat ads in the convention programs. Network anchorpersons like Dan Rather made smiling star appearances. As Richard Berke, the national political correspondent for the *New York Times*, told the National Gay and Lesbian Journalists Association: "There are times when . . . . literally three-quarters of the people deciding what's on the front page are not-so-closeted homosexuals." It's the Pink Wall of Silence. Clearly, if Brown and Carpenter had been the *victims* of violence, instead of the perpetrators of violence, their story would have been front-page news.

Example Two: After his death Allen Ginsberg, the renowned Beat poet, was eulogized across the land. Ginsberg had been openly gay and the gay community was proud to call him one of their own. Curiously, not one story about Mr. Ginsberg included any mention of that dimension of his psychology that the average Joe or Jane would have found most striking: Ginsberg was an outspoken and devoted enthusiast of pederasty. He loved to have sexual relations with boys.

Ginsberg was a lifetime member of NAMBLA, the North American Man-Boy Love Association, a group of gay men who vigorously campaign for the abolition of all age-of-consent laws. Ginsberg even appeared in a documentary film about NAMBLA wherein he recited a poem in praise of pedophilia. Ginsberg used his considerable talent to create poem after poem about the thrill of man-boy romance. To quote Leland Stevenson, another NAMBLA member: "Ginsberg certainly was interested in teenage boys. This was obvious. He wrote about it and rhapsodized about it. It was something he supported, something he considered a positive human value."

And yet there was not so much as a peep in the press about Ginsberg's lust for youngsters. Again, this is because the people in America's pressrooms and broadcast studios are complicit in the promotion of a radical gay social agenda. The news you are allowed to see, hear and read has been censored, spun, filtered and sanitized to ensure that the public image of certain protected groups is always cosmetically enhanced to politically-correct perfection.

When seen through the distorting lens of liberal-left ideology, concerned parents become anti-gay bigots, an advocate of pederasty becomes a smiling gay icon and a gay couple who rape and kill a nice boy become "local news" and are given protective cover by the liberal press. One thing is certain: you aren't being shown the full panorama of gay behavior, you are only allowed to

peek through a keyhole that liberal editors have created. It's
enough to make a normal person disgusted.

Chapter Eight

Setting the Stage for One-Sex Wedlock

Lawrence vs. Texas

On September 17, 1998, in response to a citizen report of an armed intruder "going crazy," Harris County deputies rushed to 794 Normandy St., in Houston. When they arrived at the apartment of John Geddes Lawrence the door was unlocked, so the police entered the eighth-floor apartment and began to search for the gunman. The cops found no gunman, but the cops did find 55-year-old John Geddes Lawrence enthusiastically violating the Texas sodomy statutes with Tyron Garner, who was 24 years his junior.

The randy duo were taken from the apartment in their underwear. They spent 24 hours cooling off in jail. They were later fined $200 each plus an additional $141.25 in court costs. Mr. Lawrence's prankish neighbor, Roger Nance, would spend 15 days in the slammer for filing a bogus crime report.

The Lambda Legal Defense Fund would later defend Lawrence and Garner before the Supreme Court. What bugged these gay lawyers the most was the fact that twenty-six years before, in 1972, when Texas revised its penal code, heterosexual sodomy and bestiality were dropped as criminal offenses in Texas. Only homosexual anal intercourse remained in the statute. If the cops had stumbled upon John Lawrence stark naked between satin sheets doing the Big Nasty with a Rottweiler, all they could have done was suggest that he choose a sex partner of his own species. It seemed wrong to the Lambda lawyers that Lawrence and Garner were being penalized just because they wanted to play Rump Ranger with each other.

At that moment nine states had sodomy laws that prohibited consensual sodomy for everyone: Alabama, Florida, Idaho, Louisiana, Mississippi, North Carolina, South Carolina, Utah and Virginia. Another four states, Texas, Kansas, Oklahoma and

Missouri, had statutes that forbade oral and anal sex between persons of the same sex. None of these laws were regularly enforced. Lawrence and Garner had pleaded no contest at their trial, which left the door open for an appeal of their conviction. After losing a subsequent appeal in a Texas court, the matter was appealed again and finally came for consideration before the United States Supreme Court, where it was officially dubbed *Lawrence and Garner vs. Texas.*

The Lawrence Decision

Based on early arguments on behalf of Lawrence and Garner, it appeared that the court would take the socially least disruptive path and decide the case on the basis of the Constitution's guarantee of equal protection before the law. It was anticipated that the court would simply say that Texas law could not punish homosexuals who performed sex acts that were not violations of the law when performed by heterosexuals. That's all the court needed to do. No precedents would have been set; no established law would have been overturned. Such a simple decision would have sidestepped the deeper question of the constitutional status of homosexual rights. Nonetheless, the very fact that the Supreme Court was even considering such a case only seventeen years after it had dismissed as "facetious" the very idea that a constitutional right to privacy extended to private homosexual sex acts lent an air of tension to the courtroom, which was packed with the elite corps of Washington's gay and lesbian lawyers, who had filled all the seats reserved for the Supreme Court bar by 6:30 A.M. for the 11 o'clock arguments.

When the arguments began it was clear that the two advocates were a mismatch. The advocate for Lawrence and Garner was Paul M. Smith, a former Supreme Court law clerk whose assured presentation was the result of years of experience. Mr. Smith, an openly gay lawyer, had been before the court in eight previous cases. He was unperturbed even while sparring with Antonin Scalia. By contrast, Charles A. Rosenthal Jr., the district attorney from Harris County, was in this arena for the first time. He seemed surprised by questions that he should have anticipated. He seemed not to comprehend the repeated offers of help extended to him by Justice Scalia. During his oration the frustrated justices finally resorted to sparring with one another while ignoring Mr. Rosenthal. All of the justices queried Mr. Smith, but 23 of the 35 questions asked of him came from Justice Scalia. Eight of the justices appeared content to let the colloquies between Mr. Smith and Justice Scalia showcase the issues.

Justice Scalia was clearly unimpressed by Mr. Smith's arguments. Mr. Smith argued that a homosexual's right to indulge in homosexual acts privately might be rooted in a cantankerous libertarian spirit of personal privacy dating back to the nation's beginnings. He remained silent about the fact that America has always maintained anti-sodomy statutes. Mr. Smith drew attention to the repeal of anti-sodomy statutes in three-fourths of the states as evidence of an emerging social consensus on sodomy; he argued that such statutes were "not consistent with our basic American values," to which Justice Scalia responded: "Well, it depends on what you mean by basic American values. Suppose that all the states had laws against flagpole sitting at one time," and subsequently repealed them. "Does that make flagpole sitting a fundamental right?"

In the aggregate, the arguments were far from exhaustive. Mr. Smith completed his argument in a mere thirty minutes. All arguments began and ended on March 26, 2003. Ninety days later, on June 26th, the nine justices made public their decision and opinions. The courtroom was packed with people habituated to the most far-flung sexual appetites; their mood was wavering between expectation and apprehension. Then Justice Kennedy began to speak. The gay and lesbian lawyers were the first to show signs of relief; by the time Kennedy began expounding about the dignity and respect that homosexuals deserve, some of the inverts in the audience were weeping with joy.

The breadth of the majority decision was startling. The justices, all of them near 70 years of age, had become engrossed in the nature of human sexuality. They also revealed an unanticipated attentiveness to the changing legal fashions beyond America's borders and a concern that the United States was not keeping pace with new European social trends. Justice Kennedy cited a 1981 gay rights opinion by the European Court of Human Rights which was the first citation of any decision by that court in a Supreme Court majority decision. Justice Scalia criticized this novel invocation as evidence of some sort of Western consensus on sexual privacy; he cautioned that the Supreme Court should not infuse foreign sensibilities into American constitutional law.

As recently as 1986 the Supreme Court had held that Georgia's sodomy law, which applied equally to heterosexuals and homosexuals, did not violate any constitutionally protected right to privacy. In that majority opinion Justice Byron White opined that "to claim that a right to engage in such conduct is 'deeply rooted in this Nation's history and tradition' or 'implicit in the concept of ordered liberty' is, at best, facetious." This 1986 ruling is known as *Bowers vs. Hardwick*, and the majority decision held that the Constitution does not implicitly protect a right to engage in unrestricted private consensual sexual high jinx. The court's ruling in *Lawrence v. Texas* overturned *Bowers vs. Hardwick* and with it every other anti-sodomy statute in America.

Based on little more than personal sentiment, six of the Supreme Court justices laid the cornerstone of an American gay social agenda. Liberal columnist E.J. Dionne called Justice Kennedy's opinion "a Magna Carta of gay rights." The justices' eloquent and effusive embrace of people with splinter-group sexual proclivities was better suited to a legislature than a courtroom, but Kennedy is not a legislator, he is a judge, and a judge is supposed to point to some justification in the Constitution for his decisions. Instead, Kennedy propped up his decision with a rubber crutch he called "substantive due process," which was no more than a deliberate contortion of constitutional verbiage about "due process" in an effort to fabricate new rights out of thin air. By using non-legal values to decide this case, Justice Kennedy undermined the constitutional order that sustains our republic.

Sandra Day O'Connor observed that Texas treats the same conduct differently based solely on whether the participants are gay or straight. O'Connor agreed that the Texas law should be voided based on the Equal Protection Clause, but she stated her belief that the Georgia law (Bowers) should not have been overruled. This was sensible. But the majority opinion relied on the Due Process Clause of the Fourteenth Amendment which reads: "No state shall . . . deprive any person of life, liberty, or property, without due process of law." The Texas penal code does impose constraints on liberty, but so do laws against prostitution, heroin distribution, or working more than sixty hours a week in a bakery. As Justice Scalia observed, "there is no right to 'liberty' under the Due Process Clause, though today's opinion repeatedly makes that claim. The Fourteenth Amendment *expressly allows* states to deprive their citizens of 'liberty', so long as 'due process of law' is provided."

The doctrine known as "substantive due process" holds that the Due Process Clause forbids states from infringing *fundamental* liberties, unless that infringement is narrowly tailored to serve a compelling state interest. The Supreme Court has repeatedly held that only *fundamental rights* qualify for "heightened scrutiny" protection. To qualify as a fundamental right it must be "deeply rooted in this nation's history and tradition." And, as Justice Scalia observed, "All other liberty interests may be abridged or abrogated pursuant to a validly enacted state law if that law is rationally related to a legitimate state interest."

The Bowers decision held that laws against homosexual sodomy do not warrant heightened scrutiny because such laws do not involve any fundamental right under the Due Process Clause. Indeed, the Bowers decision noted that the proscription against homosexual sodomy had ancient roots and that sodomy was a criminal offense at common law and was forbidden by the laws of all the original thirteen states when they ratified the Bill of Rights. In deciding the Bowers case the Supreme Court rightly concluded that a right to indulge in anal intercourse was not "deeply rooted in this nation's history and tradition." The Lawrence decision did not overrule this position. Nowhere in the Lawrence decision do the justices describe homosexual sodomy as a "fundamental right" or a "fundamental liberty interest" that might subject the Texas law to heightened scrutiny. Instead, the court contended that the Texas law failed a "rational-basis" test.

The Court made the claim, unsupported by any citations, that anti-sodomy laws do not seem to have been enforced against adults acting in private, to which Justice Scalia responded with the observation that sodomy is rarely performed on stage. "If all the Court means by 'acting in private' is 'on private premises, with the doors closed and the windows covered,' it is entirely unsurprising that evidence of enforcement would be hard to come by . . . Surely, that lack of evidence would not sustain the proposition that consensual sodomy on private premises with the doors closed and windows covered was regarded as a 'fundamental right,' even though all other consensual sodomy was criminalized." He went on to cite the hundreds of prosecutions for sodomy from 1880 to 1995, as well as 20 prosecutions and four executions during the colonial period. "Bowers' conclusion that homosexual sodomy is not a fundamental right 'deeply rooted in this nation's history and tradition' is utterly unassailable," said Scalia.

Finally, Justice Scalia turned to the shallow contention that there is no rational basis for a law prohibiting homosexual sodomy. Said the justice, "This proposition is so out of accord with our jurisprudence – indeed, with the jurisprudence of *any* society we know – that it requires little discussion."

The following are quotations from Justice Antonin Scalia's dissenting opinion:

"The Texas statute undeniably seeks to further the belief of its citizens that certain forms of sexual behavior are 'immoral and unacceptable,' – the same interest furthered by criminal laws against fornication, bigamy, adultery, adult incest, bestiality, and obscenity. Bowers held that this *was* a legitimate state interest. The Court today reaches the opposite conclusion. The Texas statute, it says 'furthers *no legitimate state interest* which can justify its intrusion into the personal and private life of the individual.' The Court embraces instead Justice Stevens' declaration in his Bowers dissent, that 'the fact that the governing majority as a State has traditionally viewed a particular practice as immoral is not a sufficient reason for upholding a law prohibiting the practice.' This effectively decrees the end of all morals legislations. If, as the Court asserts, the promotion of majoritarian sexual morality is not even a *legitimate* state interest, none of the above-mentioned laws can survive rational-basis review.

Today's opinion is the product of a Court, which is the product of a law-profession culture, that has largely signed on to the so-called homosexual agenda, by which I mean the agenda promoted by some homosexual activists directed at eliminating the moral opprobrium that has traditionally attached to homosexual conduct .
. . .

"One of the most revealing statements in today's opinion is the Court's grim warning that the criminalization of homosexual conduct is 'an invitation to subject homosexual persons to discrimination both in the public and in the private spheres.' It is clear from this that the Court has taken sides in the culture war, departing from its role of assuring, as neutral observer, that the democratic rules of engagement are observed. Many Americans do not want persons who openly engage in homosexual conduct as partners in their business, as scoutmasters for their children, as teachers in their children's schools, or as boarders in their home. They view this as protecting themselves and their families from a lifestyle that they believe to be immoral and destructive. The Court views it as 'discrimination' which it is a function of our judgments to deter. So imbued is the Court with the law profession's anti-anti-homosexual culture, that it is seemingly unaware that the attitudes of that culture are not obviously 'mainstream;' that in most states what the Court calls 'discrimination' against those who engage in homosexual acts is perfectly legal; that proposals to ban such 'discrimination' under Title VII have repeatedly been rejected by Congress; that in some cases such "discrimination" is a constitutional right . . . What Texas has chosen to do is well within the range of traditional democratic action, and its hand should not be stayed through the invention of a brand-new 'constitutional right' by a Court that is impatient of democratic change. It is indeed true that 'later generations can see that laws once thought necessary and proper in fact serve only to oppress' and when that happens, later generations can repeal those laws. But it is the premise of our system that those judgments are to be made by the people, and not imposed by a governing caste that knows best . . ."

In short, a rogue court, functioning as a band of philosopher kings, had planted its boot heel squarely in the face of America's people and the people's elected representatives. Not content to simply even things up with a simple Equal Protection argument, the architects of the majority decision chose to strike a pose as judicial activists, as forward thinkers, as avatars of avant-garde judicial fashion. They wanted to be *modern* jurists or, better yet, post-modern jurists. They wanted backward America to catch up to fashionable Europe. Within minutes of the Court's 6-to-3 decision, homosexuals were dancing on the courthouse steps and planning celebrations in forty cities. The Lambda Defense Fund called it "the most significant ruling ever for gay rights." The ruling struck down anti-sodomy laws in 13 southern and western states.

From all the hyperbole that floated around this case you might imagine that the Texas law had wrought a reign of terror on the queer folk. Justice Anthony Kennedy had intoned: "liberty protects the person from unwarranted government intrusions into a dwelling or other private places." Why he said this is anyone's guess. The police had probable cause to enter John Lawrence's unlocked apartment; they had received an eyewitness report of a gunman "going crazy." Under these circumstances the cops didn't need a warrant to enter the apartment. In their search the police stumbled upon two nominally adult males who were violating a statute. It was an awkward moment for everyone; the cops felt compelled to do their duty.

The arrest of Lawrence and Garner was the result of an extremely rare happenstance. They were the only two homosexuals *ever* to be convicted under the Texas sodomy statute in Harris County. In Texas, homosexual conduct was a mere class C misdemeanor, which is the lowest ranking prohibition that Texas has. The authorities in other states said that the Lawrence ruling would have little impact on day-to-day law enforcement because the anti-sodomy statutes were so seldom used. Virtually all arrests of

64

homosexuals, *as homosexuals*, are for public lewdness and performing sex acts *in public.* The lewdness statutes, which apply equally to both homosexuals and heterosexuals, were not affected by the Lawrence ruling.

So why was there celebration by homosexuals over the disappearance of a few laws that were rarely enforced? The answer lies in the tone and texture of the Court's majority opinion. According to the *New York Times* (6/27/03) "Gay activists . . . called the ruling the most significant legal victory in the gay rights movement, likening the decision to the seminal civil rights case, Brown v. Board of Education. They predicted it would embolden the movement…" The *Times* went on: "Activists and scholars said that by essentially acknowledging gay relationships as legitimate, the Supreme Court justices gave the gay rights movement new credibility in debates about marriage, partner benefits, adoption and parental rights." Said Paula Ettelbrick, executive director of the International Gay and Lesbian Human Rights Commission: 'The court has put gay people in the mainstream of society for the first time.'"

Clearly, what the Court had done was to take the so-called right to privacy, a right which is nowhere explicit in the Constitution and was "discovered" by the Court itself, and place it above the long established standards of community morality, human customs and religious laws that encode thousands of years of human experience. Ecstatic homosexuals were now raving over a court decision that legalized their anal-erotic compulsions. Alan Van Capelle, executive director of the Empire State Pride Agenda, compared the impact of the *Lawrence* decision to New York City's Stonewall riot "that launched the gay rights movement 34 years ago today." "This is so big," said Van Capelle, "For my generation, we'll be talking about where we were when the Lawrence decision came down."

Only days after the court decision came the kick off of the 34th annual Gay Pride Parade. A jubilant crowd had celebrated the night before in Sheridan Square near the Stonewall bar. According to Eric Tucker, a writer for the Associated Press, "The parade commemorates the Stonewall riots of 1969, when patrons of a gay bar in Greenwich Village fought back against a police raid." Mr. Tucker's reportage is a prime example of the sort of cozy faux history that undergirds contemporary gay mythology. The truth is, there never was a police raid on the Stonewall bar and there never were any heroic bar patrons who resisted anti-gay police oppression. Not a single one. What really happened was this: Early one morning, before the Stonewall was open for business, a building inspector arrived at the Stonewall to make a routine code-violation inspection. The lone inspector was accompanied by a policeman. During the inspection, someone in the bar exchanged words with the policeman and their altercation spilled out into the early morning sunlight where several unemployed transvestites were lounging about. Like chimps in a Jane Goodall documentary, these males in feminine attire began defending one of their own by pelting the policeman with rocks and trash. The policeman radioed for assistance. His reinforcement arrived. Matters worsened as both sides committed more troops to the fray. From beginning to end the so-called "Stonewall uprising" was a minor, squalid altercation, one of countless demimonde disturbances in the Big City.

What made Stonewall "different" was the zeitgeist. The notion of "gay rights" had been floating in the air for some time and the Stonewall brawl presented an opportunity to focus public attention on the aspirations of homosexuals and others with unconventional sexual proclivities. New York City's ultra-Left-all-the-time radio station, WBAI, played up the seedy Stonewall disturbance as though it were the storming of the Bastille. Gay activists west of the Hudson River say it was another five years before they first heard of Stonewall. Nonetheless, current gay mythology holds that the modern gay movement sprang from Stonewall. It's not true, but that's what every media hack is constrained by political correctness to tell you.

The rock and bottle throwers of 1969 now call themselves the Stonewall Veterans Association and they carried a banner in the Gay Pride Parade. On the streets of New York, Mayor Bloomberg pandered to the gay vote. He smiled; he waved the rainbow flag; he posed for photographs with a middle-aged transvestite in a platinum-blond wig, stars-and-stripes dress with plunging neckline, red fishnet stockings and faux-diamond encrusted sunglasses. Said the gay guy of the mayor: "He's not bad at all with drag queens."

After three decades, the New York gay parade and its clones in Chicago, Atlanta, Seattle, Minneapolis and San Francisco have become a predictable river of feather boas, rainbow wigs, rhinestone tiaras, leather, pink spandex, stiletto heels, thongs, rubber fetish wear and in-your-face nudity. It's the way gay Americans choose to present themselves to the rest of America. Observed Maria-Elena Grant of the Lavender Light Gospel Choir, "In a sense it's more important than ever to say that we're here and we're queer." In San Francisco, the ever popular lesbian exhibitionists known as Dykes on Bikes rumbled along on their motorcycles, their bare breasts bobbing in the breeze. They were followed by some quieter gay guys pedaling tricycles who billed themselves as Mikes on Trikes.

Known officially as New York City's Lesbian, Gay, Bisexual, Transgender Pride March, the parade lasted five hours and flowed from Fifth Avenue at 52nd Street down to the West Village where it ended at Greenwich and Christopher Streets. Shouting through a megaphone, Senator Charles Schumer (D-NY) bellowed "Let's even hear it for the Supreme Court – who ever thought we'd say that?"

Marty Downs, a community organizer with the New York Lesbian, Gay, Bisexual and Transgender Community Center, said, "There's such a response, such a sense of movement. This year, it feels really political." Tom Ammiano, who was one of two candidates campaigning to become the first gay mayor of San Francisco, remarked, "We got a couple of breaks in the last few weeks, with Canada legalizing gay marriage and now the Supreme Court. It looks like Sandra Day O'Connor watching "Will & Grace" really paid off." Homosexual activists predicted that the Lawrence decision would pave the way to same-sex marriage. As lesbian Lisa Sbrana saw it, "It gives us legitimacy for marriages and adoption."

It was probably no coincidence that the Lawrence decision came only three days before the annual gay festivities: the liberals on the Supreme Court were intent on changing the fabric of American society.

Chapter Nine

The Gay Agenda

In 1987 two homosexual strategists, Marshall Kirk and Hunter Madsen, laid the groundwork for the normalization of gay counter-cultural values in their seminal essay *The Overhauling of Straight America.* In this essay the authors exhorted their gay compatriots to desensitize the public to the point that Americans would "view homosexuality with indifference instead of keen emotion." If this could be accomplished, the authors assured the gay community, their battle to mainstream gay behavior was "virtually won." The authors called for a "large-scale media campaign" to "change the image of gays in America." They proposed a six-point agenda.

First of all, they admonished their fellow travelers to "Talk about gays and gayness as loudly and as often as possible." Their theory was that relentless chatter about this sexually deviant 1% of the population would make homosexual behavior seem commonplace, even normal. They instructed gays to "use talk to muddy the moral waters" when people with religious convictions had moral objections. They encouraged homosexuals to curry favor with liberal churches and then use this support to undermine the moral authority of traditional churches. They urged gays to spin-doctor biblical teachings and portray traditionalists as backwoods hicks who are hopelessly out of touch with the latest moral fashions.

Point two of their explicit agenda was to "Portray gays as victims, not as aggressive challengers." These clever propagandists noted that "In any campaign to win over the public, gays must be cast as victims in need of protection so that straights will be included by reflex to assume the role of protector." In the twenty-seven years since this essay was written this gay-agenda goal has found expression in countless public school "safe zones," classrooms where students who have questions about their sexuality can go to talk to teachers who may then refer them to gay activist groups for counseling without parental notification or consent. The acceptance of this propagandistic news slant also explains why the slaying of gay Matthew Shepherd held the attention of newspapers for months, while the brutal kidnapping, rape and murder of Jesse Dirkhising by homosexuals was deemed simply not newsworthy.

Kirk and Madsen acknowledged that homosexuals were not likely to make much social headway by seeking direct support for homosexual practices. Instead they suggested that gays play up the anti-discrimination angle, which would work well with the "gays as victims" theme set forth above. They instructed gays to "give protectors just cause" and to portray all those who opposed them as brainless bigots. This was point three of their agenda.

Point four was to "Make gays look good." Gays should be portrayed as solid citizens; the less said about flaming drag queens and fisting orgies in leather bars, the better. Making gays look good has been a preoccupation at the *New York Times* since the Lawrence decision. Glowing profiles of gay lovers and gay parents are now a staple at the *Times*.

The fifth objective of this gay manifesto is to "Make the victimizers look bad." By "victimizer" they mean anyone who would dream of objecting to their unraveling of the nation's moral fabric. Here the two visionaries become more strident: "At a later stage of the media campaign for gay rights – long after other gay ads have become commonplace – it will be time to get tough with remaining opponents. To be blunt, they must be vilified…Our goal here is twofold. First, we seek to replace the mainstream's self-righteous pride about its homophobia with shame and guilt. Second, we intend to make the anti-gays look so nasty that average Americans will want to dissociate themselves from such types."

They go on to detail the sorts of imagery that might be used to best effect in their late-stage propaganda campaign. The opposition to the gay social agenda, they suggest, should be depicted as Ku Klux Klansmen, "drooling" southern ministers, punks, thugs and convicts. They suggest a follow-up tour of Nazi concentration camps. Anyone who gets in their way will be stigmatized as comical or deranged or a menace.

The final objective of Kirk-and-Madsen's agenda is fund raising: "Solicit Funds." Propaganda machines run on money, so they offer fund raising suggestions. Thousands of organizations, websites and school programs now promote this six-point program, sometimes openly but often in disguised forms.

So, we need wonder no longer: there *is* a gay social agenda, an explicit plan to mainstream the homosexual subculture and the behavioral habits that are peculiar to it.

The Gay, Lesbian and Straight Education Network (GLSEN) has a working budget of 3.5 million dollars. Its purpose is to shape the moral values of American school children. It has become a powerful force in American schools and it too has a written agenda; it is titled *Institutionalized Heterosexism in Our Schools: A Guide to Understanding and Undoing It.* The Network defines heterosexism as "the belief that heterosexuality is 'normal'." In other words, even though ninety-nine percent of the world's population is inclined toward heterosexuality, you are a pig-headed heterosexist bigot if you believe that heterosexuality is normal. This is what passes for rationality in the gay community.

At their 1999 GLSEN convention in Atlanta, speakers outlined their battle plan. GLSEN's communications director, James Anderson, announced: "We're going to raise a generation of kids who don't believe the religious right." In case anyone missed the point, Deanna Duby of the National Education Association hit the nail on the head when she affirmed that "the schools of today are the governments of tomorrow." So the NEA is in bed with the gay activists.

In 2000 the same Gay, Lesbian and Straight Education Network, together with the Massachusetts Education Department, sponsored a TeachOUT at Tufts University in Boston. Their purpose was to teach public school teachers how to weave lots of positive messages about homosexuality into their classroom instruction. The instruction included how to enlighten your kids about homosexual behaviors, including the ever-popular "fisting": stuffing one's fist into another person's rectum.

Not to be outdone, a Newton South High School teacher, in Newton, Massachusetts, described to the *Boston Globe* how he worked "bisexual, gay, lesbian and transgendered" material into his classroom instruction. He handed out copies of Stephen Chbosky's *The Perks of Being a Wallflower* and insisted that his students write essays about it. This novel showcases such frolicsome fun as boy-dog anal intercourse, hot pumpin' man-boy sex, anal intercourse between boys, male masturbation, and throbbing female masturbation with a hot dog. A parent who took exception to all this was dismissed as a moralizing heterosexist. Every public school in America is now a target of opportunity for infiltration by agents committed to the gay agenda.

So, the gay social agenda exists, it is explicit, it has written manifestos, it is in full swing, it is well funded, and it has the support of influential organizations, including a large and dedicated following among America's public school teachers. We can see clearly now that all of those snide portrayals of Justice Scalia as some sort of right-wing rustic for merely referring to the "so-called gay rights agenda" were just a smokescreen to mask the fact that there **is** an aggressive and invasive gay social agenda that is reshaping America.

Strange Biology

Much of what aspires to be a debate over the issue of homosexual wedlock appears to be little more than an exchange of brickbats. The gay lobby calls its opponents "backward" and the traditionalists call the homosexuals "sinful". Much of this exchange takes place in letters to editors and emotional ventilations on talk radio. A closer consideration of these exchanges reveals the presence of primitive proto-arguments.

By calling the traditionalists backward, the gay lobby means to convey their reading of history; they see society as gradually progressing from treating homosexuals as criminals, to treating them as medical patients, to treating them as merely queer, as odd but unthreatening fellow humans. The next logical step in this progression, as they see it, is full acceptance and full integration into society's institutions, including matrimony. People who don't share this vision of progressive social evolution are imagined to be blind, uneducated and standing in the way of History.

When traditionalists call homosexuals sinful they are trying to convey one of several things, depending upon which tradition they are defending. The biblical traditionalists see themselves, and people like themselves, as the bedrock of a well-ordered society; they look to Leviticus as a reminder of what they are **not**. They are definitely **not** "sodomites," and this shared vision of themselves gives their vision of society a solid center. Living consistently in adherence to tradition is understood to be a force for social cohesion which serves to preserve civilization. Any behaviors that threaten this social cohesion meet the traditionalist's definition of sinful.

The word sin was originally an ancient Aramaic archery term; it meant, literally, to miss the mark. Many traditionalists use the word sinful in exactly this sense to convey their perception that homosexuals have wandered off the well-worn path of sensible, or even sane, conduct. Why would they see homosexuals this way? The most obvious reason is the queerness of homosexual behavior. The internal emotional compass that guides homosexuals points *away* from the emotional magnetic north that orients ninety-nine percent of humanity.

Homosexuals insist that they "were born this way," that their homosexuality is inborn and therefore "natural." We are left to infer that because their homosexuality is so "natural" that it must also be "good," and a purposeful part of Mother Nature's rainbow coalition. It's a weak argument. Nature is replete with oddities, each in its own niche, which is not bad, but not "good" either; they are just *odd*.

Scientific evidence supports the testimony of gays that some gayness emerges from a constellation of proclivities that have their origins in the fine-grained neurologies and chemistries that are peculiar to homosexual humans. But there is no standard homosexual. Homosexuality may result from genetic mutations or from exposure to the wrong hormone during fetal development. Cultural influences, personal experiences and organic defects, such as an inability to produce or respond to one's own hormones, will also shape the final expression of sexuality. There are, in short, a variety of homosexualities, all of which are the result of abnormal development. Sometimes things go haywire. Take, for example, lesbians.

Where Do Lesbians Come From?

Both sexes are genetically coded to become either males or females. During the development of a normal male human the little fellow's genetic code triggers the development of testes, which soon begin secreting the powerful and formative hormone testosterone. This hormone shapes the neurological architecture of the developing male so that at birth his body (morphology) and his natural proclivities (neurology) complement one another. It is this complementary relation between body and psyche that makes him a normal human male.

Normal female humans follow a similar path, with the exception that their genetic codes dictate the development of female organs and the secretion of female hormones. The normal female human has a neurology (psyche) that complements her morphology.

The key to unlocking the mystery of lesbian creation is this one simple fact: the bodies of both sexes produce both estrogen and testosterone, though in very different proportions. If the body of a woman were to secrete an excessive amount of testosterone while she was pregnant with a daughter, then the mother's testosterone would have the same formative effect on her developing daughter's developing neurology that a male fetus' testosterone has on his developing neurology. This daughter is more likely to be born a morphological female, but with a quasi-male neurology. Scholarly papers coyly referred to such offspring as "tomboys" as long ago as the 1960s.

The mismatched conjoining of female morphology and quasi-male neurology raises a provocative question: are lesbians women?

74

They are convincingly female in appearance, but are they *women*? The words "female" and "human" are biological categories, but the word "woman" designates a *cultural* category. Within any culture, what makes a female a woman is her embrace of certain *culturally defined* feminine virtues. Without this core of feminine virtues a female does not achieve womanhood in the estimation of traditional culture. She may lack beauty, or brilliance, or fertility and still be a vessel of feminine virtue and therefore a woman. Conversely, a female may be beautiful, brilliant and fertile and still be so queer in her appetites and inclinations as to have stumbled beyond the borders of her culture's definition of what a woman truly is. This is one reason why lesbian marriage feels so alien; not only is there no man in the union, there are no *women* in it either. Therefore, every "gay marriage" is a *caricature* of traditional marriage, an institutional gargoyle emerging from a corrupted biology.

Advertisements for an Alien Culture

Now that Marshall Kirk and Hunter Madsen have specifically enumerated the battle plan of homosexual activism we can more clearly identify the motivations of writers in the popular press. The *New York Times* has been preeminent in its promotion of the gay agenda; the *Times* has followed the Kirk/Madsen strategy to the letter. Since the *Lawrence v. Texas* decision the *New York Times* has been unswerving in its vigorous promotion of homosexual marriage. Not a week passes without some charming profile of some flawlessly endearing gay person or gay couple. Sometimes three such articles appear in a single issue of the *Times*. It's really sort of creepy. Meet the Stepford Gays . . .

On January 12, 2004 the *New York Times* put an article titled *Two Fathers, With One Happy to Stay at Home* on its front page. It was a mash note to homosexual fatherhood. We are told that "The obstacles to finding surrogate mothers and of discriminatory adoption laws that favor heterosexual couples have led some gay men to pursue parenthood with fervor." The article avoids nettlesome questions about *why* surrogate moms and adoption experts might "discriminate" against homosexual couples.

The *Times* writer evinces not a bit of curiosity about these things. The article is about how *superior* gay stay-at-home males are when compared with mere mothers: "Of the 9,328 same-sex couples with children whose census returns were randomly selected for analysis by the Census Bureau, 26 percent of the male couples included a stay-at-home parent...That figure is one percent more than for married couples with children."

According to the 2000 census, only 20 percent of male couples and a third of female couples live in households with children. The total of all such households does not exceed 156,000, which is microscopic when compared to the vast heterosexual majority. Remember, gays are only 1% of the population to begin with. The true purpose of this article was to highlight points one and four of the Kirk & Madsen gay agenda: "Talk about gays and gayness as loudly and as often as possible" and "Make gays look good."

On Tuesday, December 16, 2003 the *Times* devoted 42 column inches to telling the heart-warming story of Elmer Lokkins, 84, and Gustavo Archilla, 88, "who hid their sexual orientation for 58 years." The article is titled "They Held Out for Marriage" and subtitled "After 6 Decades of Decorum in Public, Gus and Elmer Eloped." Yup! They "crossed the Canadian border near Niagara Falls and were married." The *Times* got right to the point: "The couple capture what some in the gay rights movement say is an essential but unappreciated point in the argument for same-sex marriage: it offers something more basic and profound than survivor rights and shared health care. For gays and lesbians, the power of marriage lies in the sanctity of its tradition, its *social legitimacy*..." [Emphasis added] In no sense was this newspaper article *news*. It is a mood piece intended to talk about gayness, to make gayness seem normal, to "make gays look good."

The first page of the *Times* Metro Section (12/20/03) showcased a glowing profile of a lesbian couple titled "More Than Mere Partners" and subtitled "By Example, Lesbian Couple Try to State Case for Marriage." Actually, it's the *New York Times* that is trying to state the case. The writer, Andrew Jacobs, goes through comical contortions to make two sexual inverts seem non-

76

threatening. In the very first paragraph we are told that "there is nothing flamboyant about the Kilian-Meneghin household" and that there are "Norman Rockwell figurines in the beige-on-brown living room." We are assured that one of the lesbians is "soft-spoken" and the other one is "nerdy." We are soothed by the knowledge that they "have a pair of exceedingly polite children" and "an elderly cat named Spot." In case we missed his point, Mr. Jacobs drives it home by telling us that "By most standards, the family is as all-American and unremarkable as they come." That's just the first paragraph.

Eventually the writer gets around to telling us that these two females are plaintiffs in a lawsuit "that has turned New Jersey into the next battleground in the war over same-sex marriage." Guess which side the *Times* is on? We hear from Ms. Kilian's boss who says of the lesbians, "They're worse than Ozzie and Harriet...They're the most boring people I've ever met." Translation: these gays are *non-threatening*. These lesbians drag their kids to news conferences and photo ops where son Joshua obligingly chirps "Everyone knows we're a fun family!" Both lesbians became pregnant with the assistance of sperm banks, one of the techniques known in lesbian street parlance as "sperm trapping."

It is now standard practice for articles about homosexuals that have *no news value* to be used to "talk about gays and gayness" and to "muddy the moral waters" and to "portray gays as victims" and to "make gays look good." The *New York Times* is slavishly following the black-letter script of Kirk & Madsen's gay political agenda. Surely anyone who would stand in the way of these two Ozzie-and-Harriet, soft-spoken-and-nerdy, "all-American and unremarkable" collectors of Norman Rockwell figurines **must** be a heartless monster. That's the hidden liberal-media message.

In the estimation of the far-Left "progressives," you are a monster if you question the social implications of one-sex wedlock. And yet, there is that nagging phrase from the first paragraph of the *Times* article: "By most standards the family is all-American and unremarkable." Let's look a bit closer at that sentence.

Small flaws can produce dire consequences. It's the profoundly *non-standard* dimensions of gay relationships and behaviors that should hold our attention. Articles such as these are masterpieces of misdirection; they are designed to distract our attention from the very things to which it should be riveted. These are not news articles; they are advertisements for an alien culture.

An article in the *New York Times* titled "Many Successful Gay Marriages Share an Open Secret" (1/28/10) hints at what lies ahead for marriage in America. The opening line tells us that "When Rio and Ray married in 2008, the Bay Area women omitted two words from their wedding vows: fidelity and monogamy." In a supportive voice the *New York Times* tells us that these two middle-aged lesbians "knew from the beginning that their bond would be forged on their own terms, including what they call 'play' with other women."

After that insightful anecdote the *Times* directs our attention to a study "offering a rare glimpse inside gay relationships and reveals that monogamy is not a central feature for many . . . New research at San Francisco State University reveals just how common open relationships are among gay men and lesbians in the Bay Area. The Gay Couples Study has followed 556 male couples for three years – about 50 percent of those surveyed have sex outside their relationships, with the knowledge and approval of their partners.

"That consent is key. 'With straight people, it's called affairs and cheating,' said Colleen Hoff, the study's principal investigator, 'but with gay people it does not have such negative connotations.'"

And:

"None of this is news in the gay community, but few will speak publicly about it. Of the dozen people in open relationships contacted for this column, no one would agree to use his or her full name, citing privacy concerns. They also worried that discussing the subject could undermine the legal fight for same-sex marriage." Gee, why would they think that?

Why this is "news" to anyone is anyone's guess. When the typical male homosexual (age 37) reports having had an average of 500 different sex partners, any expectation of monogamous behavior by homosexuals is delusional. The only reason this study is a "rare glimpse" into gay moral values is because the *New York Times* and its imitators have taken a vow of allegiance to "make gays look good" in accordance with the media script written for them by Marshall Kirk and Hunter Madsen.

The *Times* introduces us to Chris and James who were wed at San Francisco's City Hall and then "opened their relationship a year ago after concluding that they were not fully meeting each other's needs. But they have rules: complete disclosure, honesty about all encounters, advance approval of partners, and no sex with strangers – they must know the other men first. 'We check in with each other on this an awful lot,' said James, 37.'" This arrangement is a foreshadowing of homosexual plural marriage; it is *very* communal.

The *Times* included the aptly named Joe Quirk, author of a "relationship book" titled "It's Not You, It's Biology" as one of its chosen "experts." Joe is all for "freedom" and "transparency."

"The traditional American marriage is in crisis, and we need insight," says Joe, citing the fresh perspective that gay couples bring to matrimony. "If innovation in marriage is going to occur, it will be spearheaded by homosexual marriages."

The *New York Times* is all for "marriage innovation." Based on some undisclosed moral code unknown to any human culture in recorded history, the *New York Times* enthusiastically endorses similar homosexual households as fit environments in which to raise children who were otherwise destined to become healthy heterosexuals.

A similar study by the University of Vermont revealed that only half of male couples who entered civil unions in 2000-2001 believed that monogamy was something to be valued. Popular gay commentator Dan Savage declares that "Gay male couples don't view monogamy as a defining characteristic of a loving, committed relationship." Since gay males outnumber lesbians threefold, it will be these gay-male relationships that define the essence of "gay marriage" in contradistinction to our traditional marriage culture. Heterosexual couples don't *begin* their marriages with the expectation of sexual entanglements with outsiders.

This dismissive attitude is echoed by Troy Perry, the founder of the Metropolitan Christian Churches, a cluster of gay-oriented churches. Mr. Perry tells us that "Monogamy is not a word that the gay community uses . . . Some would say that committed couples could have multiple sexual partners as long as there's no deception. Each couple has to decide." This popular gay perspective pretty much trashes the traditional definition of marriage along with a core commandment of biblical Christianity and Judaism, the one about adultery. No one in the "gay community" raised an eyebrow when the very first gay couple in line to receive a marriage license in Provincetown, Mass. gave their sought-after sentiments about marriage to an eagerly awaiting media. That's when would-be spouse Jonathan Yarbrough said, "I think it's possible to love more than one person and have more than one partner, not in the polygamist sense. In our case, it is, we have, an 'open' marriage." All of this is evidence beyond doubt that any attempt to mainstream homosexual countercultural values can only result in serious harm to our sustaining traditional marriage culture.

Most Americans have never read the *New York Times*; they have never even held an issue of the *Times* in their hands. So why should you care what they publish? Here's the reason: the publishers of newspapers across America have the *New York Times* delivered to their desks every morning. The *Times* sets the news agenda for most of the print and electronic media in America. Most of the media share the cultural biases of the *Times* editorial staff. The sensibility of the *Times* feels comfortable to the scribblers and the talking haircuts who mold public opinion in countless media markets across America. They use the *Times* as a blueprint for how they should present issues to you. So even if you have never seen a copy of the *New York Times* you do, in fact, read a version of it every day.

The propaganda campaign in support of homosexual wedlock is distinguished by the near absence of intellectual rigor. The *New York Times* and its sing-along imitators persist in repeating the same tiresome formula: they offer carefully sanitized portraits of "safe" homosexuals and then ask the rhetorical question, "What possible harm would result if Bert and Ernie were able to enter into a socially sanctioned marriage?" This presentation places the burden of the argument on society; those of us who have reservations about a radical transformation of our central organizing institutions are expected to justify our refusal to approve of homosexual wedlock.

The gay propagandists have it backwards. The burden of the argument is on *their* shoulders. Like bioengineers introducing some new genetically-altered food into the marketplace, the burden of proof is on the homosexual lobby to demonstrate to society that homosexual wedlock will not alter the existing sociosphere in ways that society will find discomfiting. Homosexuality has always been morally suspect in the opinion of every Christian society; it has no history of acceptance in Christian culture. Around 550 BC, when the Greeks were cranking out homoerotic poetry, the Jews were writing the book of Leviticus which condemned homosexual acts. Leviticus was the law. It served to order Jewish society and to differentiate Judaism from Mediterranean cults in which transvestite priests, eunuchs and various sex acts were central to cult rituals. What our wise Jewish and Christian forebears understood is that the things people refuse to do can be as important in defining who they are as a people as the things that they do. A shared social vision of ourselves as a people who **do not** indulge in certain behaviors continues to be an important force for social cohesion in our culture.

For Christian people, the homosexuality of ancient Greece was always tainted by its close association with pederasty and the power difference between adult and child. In the eyes of Christians, Roman homoerotism was tainted by its association with slavery and the power difference between the homosexual master and the powerless slave. Though the gay community imagines the ancient world to be a golden age of homoerotism, both Greek and Roman homosexuality are tainted by the element of coercion, which Christian culture finds repugnant.

Chapter Ten

Still Crazy After All These Years

Homosexuals are quick to remind everyone that the American Psychiatric Association removed homosexuality from its encyclopedia of mental disorders in 1973. We are supposed to infer from this historical footnote that homosexuality is just one more harmless human sexual variation, that psychiatry has embraced an emerging enlightenment about the gay psyche, that progressive psychiatric professionals had, at last, cast off a suffocating prejudice. In truth, the removal of homosexuality from the list of mental disorders was the result of a totally unethical collusion between a select group of APA committee members and radical gay activists. The removal of homosexuality from the APA's catalog of disorders was a purely political act.

From the first days of gay activism the promoters of the gay agenda understood that the public's perception of homosexuals as mentally disordered was an impediment to their lobbying efforts. In 1968, representatives of gay organizations began a political campaign to persuade renowned psychiatrists and the officers of mental health organizations to reclassify the entire spectrum of homosexual behaviors as healthful manifestations of human sexuality. For three years the APA's small Homosexuality Task Force collaborated closely with the Gay Activist's Alliance, the Daughters of Bilitis and the Mattachine Society, among others. Organizations with contrasting perspectives were excluded from the deliberations; persons holding contrary opinions were excluded from membership in the APA Task Force and denied even the opportunity to present contradictory evidence to the Task Force. In short, the Homosexuality Task Force was a star-chamber proceeding, a kangaroo court whose verdict was a foregone conclusion.

While the APA Task Force was preparing its bucket of whitewash, gay radicals launched an assault against any mental health professional who attempted to document homosexual aberrancy.

83

Across America psychiatrists and psychoanalysts were shouted down or bodily assaulted in public forums.

Before submitting its final report, the APA Homosexuality Task Force sent a letter to all APA member psychiatrists urging them to "vote" for dropping homosexuality from the APA's catalog of disorders. Kept secret from the members was the fact that the letter had been written and funded by the politically motivated National Gay Task Force.

Believing, falsely, that they were honoring the wishes of their own organization's elder statesmen, the members voted "yes" on the motion by a slender margin. Thereafter, the APA removed homosexuality from the 1973 edition of its *Diagnostic and Statistical Manual*.

For the first and only time in history a professional mental health organization had *voted* on the status of a mental illness. Its abrupt reversal was not based on any new scientific evidence; it was the result of a political stunt. Only 25% of the recipients of the original 1973 APA Homosexuality Task Force letter bothered to respond to it. Most members threw their ballots in the wastebasket. The tally of this skewed "vote" was, therefore, deeply flawed by "volunteer bias," the very same bias that skewed Alfred Kinsey's homosexuality studies. In retrospect, it is clear that if the silent majority of the APA membership had responded to the letter, then homosexuality would still be classified as a mental disorder.

Later surveys, which offered APA members confidentiality and freedom from the fear of radical gay retaliation, demonstrated that two-thirds of APA psychiatrists held firm in their belief that homosexuality is abnormal and aberrant. Four years after the bogus APA "vote," the journal *Medical Aspects of Human Sexuality*, published the results of a poll of 2,500 psychiatrists on the subject of homosexuality. These doctors, by a whopping 69% to 18%, confirmed that "Homosexuality was usually a pathological adaptation as opposed to a normal variation."

The curious bent of the American Psychiatric Association's leadership surfaced once again on Monday, May 19, 2003 when, at a San Francisco symposium, they suggested the possible removal from the forthcoming edition of their manual of mental disorders the following: pedophilia, exhibitionism, fetishism, transvestism, voyeurism and sadomasochism. Dr. Charles Moser argued in favor of de-pathologizing pedophilia, suggesting that there was little proof that sex with adults was harmful to minors. It was argued that society should not discriminate against adults who are attracted to children. This argument was embellished with the names of high-functioning public figures who could be classified as pedophiles. Dr. Moser and his co-author Peggy Kleinplatz concluded that, "The situation of the paraphilias at present parallels that of homosexuality in the early 1970s." In other words, the declassification of homosexuality as a mental disorder paved the way for the declassification of pedophilia as a mental disorder and sadistic sexuality as well, which only calls into deeper question the wisdom of the APA leadership. The same moral midgets who sought to normalize homosexuality are now using the very same arguments in an effort to normalize child molestation, creeps who expose their genitals in public, guys who prance around in women's underwear, sexually aroused shoe sniffers and weirdoes who get a big bang out of torturing other humans.

Interviews with APA members who voted to remove homosexuality from the APA catalog of disorders revealed that many of them were motivated by a desire to alleviate the social ostracism of homosexuals; they never doubted for a minute that gays were disordered. But their vote had the unintended consequence of lending psychiatric authority to the notion that homosexuals as a group were as mentally healthy as heterosexuals. The bogus vote and its attendant publicity also had a chilling effect on the publication of research suggesting psychological problems associated with homosexuality.

J. Michael Bailey conducted many of the famous "gay twin studies" that gay activists are fond of citing in support of their "I was born this way" statements about gayness. In the 1999 Archives of General Psychiatry, Bailey commented on three published studies of homosexuality (Fergusson, Herrell and Sandfort). He said, "These studies contain arguably the best published data on the association between homosexuality and psychopathology, and both converge on the same unhappy conclusion: homosexual people are at substantially higher risk for some forms of emotional problems, including suicide, major depression, and anxiety disorder, conduct disorder, and nicotine dependence...The strength of the new studies is their degree of control."

In a study by A.P. Bell and M.S. Weinberg (1978) the authors conclude that a major reason for gay suicide attempts was the breakup of relationships. The second most common reason was the inability of gays to accept what they have chosen to be. Because gays have more partners than heterosexuals, they also experience more breakups. Long-term gay male relationships are rarely monogamous. Gays have, on average, **four times** as many partners as heterosexuals and their suicide attempts are proportionally higher. Suicide attempts among gays are about three times more frequent than among heterosexuals. High rates of compulsive sexual behavior and drug use among gays also drive up their suicide statistics. Gays are compulsively randy; to paraphrase a notorious feminist aphorism, the typical homosexual needs a marriage like a fish needs a bicycle.

Social stigma does not appear to be the reason for homosexual mental health problems. Studies comparing the suicide rates of gays in the United States with those of gays in countries renowned for their tolerance of homosexuals, the Netherlands, New Zealand and Denmark, show no significant difference. Gays in America do not have more psychiatric problems than gays in more gay-friendly environments. In other words, gay problems spring from gay psychology.

Suffice it to say that the homosexual psyche has never been given a clean bill of health by the mental health profession. The decision to remove homosexuality from the American Psychiatric Association's manual of mental disorders was made by a splinter faction of the Association's administrators working in collusion with homosexual activists, who bolstered their star-chamber proceedings with a bogus "vote" secretly funded by gay radicals, to which a scant 25% of APA members bothered to respond. The change was purely political and done in an atmosphere of intimidation. Therefore, the APA vote to drop homosexuality from its list of mental disorders is not an argument in favor of homosexual wedlock.

Oh, Canada!

Canada never had a unifying social myth. Most modern nations of the New World were born in rebellion, but Canada is a child of the fear of revolution. Canada was patched together by lawyers who negotiated a series of deals in the 19th and 20th centuries in an effort to build a consensus among the local cultures of disparate provinces to entice them to join the loose confederation with a weak central government that we now call Canada. Canadians have turned their backs on their North American heritage and now look longingly to Europe for social models. Think of Canada as Sweden on the St. Lawrence, but with less distinctiveness. None of this keeps the Canadians from feeling vastly superior to Americans. Only the French can top the Canadians for snotty superiority.

In the 1860s, fugitive slaves fled to Canada, but soon returned to join the Union army. In the 1870s, Sitting Bull and his Sioux nation escaped the American cavalry and made Saskatchewan home for a while before returning south. Though neither group found the Canadians particularly welcoming, their presence helped the Canadians form a notion of themselves as morally superior in the way they treat minorities. "We have always prided ourselves as being the northern terminus of the Underground Railroad, so we never stop enjoying embarrassing America as inferior in race relations," said Austin Clarke, a Canadian novelist, born in Barbados. So now they can cluck their tongues about how the Americans treat homosexuals, who are imagined to be a genuine minority. Besides their shared love of ice hockey and Tim Horton doughnuts, a shared moral smugness is something for the Canadians to cling to.

The *New York Times* devoted 24 column inches to the tale of two Cleveland lesbian librarians who planned to get hitched while in Toronto for a librarian's convention. "They came to Toronto city hall this week, where the rainbow flag now flies on the roof to celebrate Pride Week and the new social revolution going on inside, and filled out a marriage license application, which still has blanks for bridegroom and bride." Fifty-six-year-old lesbian librarian Linda Chopra said she didn't expect her Canadian marriage to be recognized in Ohio. "Nevertheless," the *Times* tells us, "...she wanted to get married anyway, in part so that when her granddaughter comes to visit, 'she will have two grandmothers in the same house and know that our relationship is legally acceptable.'" Perhaps we can expect a sequel to the classroom gay-pride classic "Heather Has Two Mommies", titled "Heather Has Three Grannies," or maybe four grannies as the case may be. With gay divorce certain to follow gay marriage, poor Heather could end up knowing five or six "grandmothers" and never have known the love of a single grandfather.

Then came a *New York Times* article titled *Now Free to Marry, Canada's Gays Say, 'Do I?'* It may have been a sly attempt to make the notion of homosexual wedlock seem less threatening by suggesting that many gays didn't *really* want to marry their partners. Writing from a Toronto dateline, Clifford Krauss tells us that when 41-year-old Davis Andrew heard that a court had extended the marriage privilege to homosexuals "he broke into a sweat." Mr. Andrew recalled, "I was dreading the conversation [with my partner]. Personally, I saw marriage as a dumbing down of gay relationships. My dread is that soon you will have a complacent bloc of gay and lesbian soccer moms."
The *Times* writer adds: "His skepticism about marriage is a recurring refrain among Canadian gay couples, who have not rushed to marry in great numbers in the weeks since June 10, when they became eligible. Rather, the extension of marriage rights has thrown gays here into a heated debate, akin to the one that embroiled the American civil rights movement in the 1960's over how much 'integration' is a good thing – and what gay marriage should consist of."

The article went on to say that many gays fear that marriage and mainstreaming will erode their cherished notion of themselves as a unique people with a unique culture and history. Respectability, it seems, is a challenge to gay identity. The debate is between those who yearn for acceptance and those who celebrate a flamboyant gay counterculture. Said the *Times*: "So heated is the conversation that some gay Canadians said in interviews that they would not bring up the topic at dinner parties." The editor-in-chief of *Fab*, a popular gay magazine in Toronto, opined, "I'd be for marriage if I thought gay people would challenge and change the institution and not buy into the traditional meaning of 'till death do us part' and monogamy forever. We should be Oscar Wildes and not like everyone else watching the play." In other words, he believes that gay marriage should *threaten* the institution of marriage as it exists, should be a kind of Trojan Horse bringing with it a disrespect for monogamy and permanence. The *New York Times* observed that "gay men seem more apprehensive about marriage than lesbians..." Well, duh. Gay men outnumber lesbians by at least three to one. In addition, the average lesbian respondent claims to have had only ten homosexual encounters. This contrasts wildly with the typical gay male respondent who numbers his sexual encounters in the hundreds and still counting. Promiscuity is the hallmark of male homosexuality and because gay males dominate gay demographics, it will be the gay male sensibility that will most strongly shape the public's perception of any emerging institution of gay marriage.

Hints of the grotesque parody of traditional marriage that gay marriage will become appeared in *Fab* magazine, which caters to Canada's largest gay community. The magazine dispensed tips on bridal harnesses and blue leather garters, gay bachelor party strippers, and where to find "black magic flowers." With its emphasis on fetish wear and pagan symbolism, these trappings of gay wedlock mocked true marriage much as the Witches' Sabbaths of the Middle Ages once mocked the Latin Mass. The same issue of *Fab* included an essay by a sociologist at the University of Toronto, who warned that gay marriage could bring with it a frightening homogenization. Said Rinaldo Walcott: "I can already hear folks saying things like: 'Why are bathhouses needed?

Straights don't have them.'" He laments, "Will queers now have to live with the heterosexual forms of guilt associated with something called cheating?"

He's right to be concerned. Any widespread capacity for self-restraint, or even a sense of shame, would put a serious dent in contemporary gay culture. Among gay males, cruising for sex is universal. Anonymous, often wordless, sexual encounters are consummated in lavatories, movie theaters, parked cars, the public parks and, of course, the bathhouses. Two-thirds of gay males have contracted a least one venereal disease at least once. Almost half of white male homosexual respondents, with an average age of 37 years, reported having had at least 500 sex partners. It is upon this rickety foundation of outlandish promiscuity that the gay community expects to establish an institution of "gay marriage."

The Gay Golden Age That Never Was

In their defense of the contemporary gay culture, homosexuals fondly direct our attention to the golden age of homoerotism in classical Greece. They will rattle off the names of historical homosexuals, as if to suggest that modern gays are continuing some noble lineage. The very antiquity of Greek homoerotism seems to cast a patina of respectability over the modern gay counterculture. The openness and visibility of homosexuality in the ancient Greek culture that gifted us so much treasured philosophy, drama, mathematics, logic and ethics seems to argue for our acceptance of homosexuality in our own culture. Indeed, gays argue that if it weren't for the dark shadow that Jewish and Christian intolerance cast over gay culture, gays today would be basking in society's warm acceptance of their natural and noble homosexuality. It's a pretty thought, but it's pure hokum.

Contemporary American gay culture bears no resemblance to classical Greek culture. To suggest that it does is a slander against the Greeks. We can take our keynote from Xenophon who, quoting Socrates, asks "Do you think the man is free who is ruled by bodily pleasures and is unable to do what is best because of them?" For the Greeks the essence of manhood lay in self-mastery and restraint. By contrast, America's gay subculture is a celebration of excess. The anonymous sexual encounters that characterize gay male behavior today would have disgusted the Greeks, whose conventions proscribed certain sexual acts, extolled restraint and abhorred anonymity. They would have found modern gays contemptible.

It was the abandonment of sexual prohibition in our own culture that encouraged ever greater sensation seeking. Among gays, this quickly led to baroque elaborations of coprophilic behaviors including anus licking (anilingus) and fist fucking. To the Greeks the very idea of a man forcing his fist up another man's rectum would have been inconceivable. Among the Greeks the passive role in anal intercourse might be played by a woman or a slave, but not by another free man. Only the powerless were the recipients of anal intercourse. It was the excessive compulsions of modern sensation-seeking gays that brought the role of slave back into the homosexual repertoire.

With average gays reporting as many as 500 sex partners, it's little wonder that AIDS spread across North America in only a few years, starting with a single infected French Canadian airline attendant, whom epidemiologists call Patient Zero. He flew from city to city infecting gays during gay sex romps. He was asked to restrain himself, but he refused.

The human anus is not a genuine sex organ; it is easily lacerated; it is the perfect pathway for germ transmission. Gay male sex is uniformly unhealthy. Gay males have strikingly high instances of anal cancer. The list of diseases found with frequency among gay males as a result of their abnormal sexual appetites includes Chlamydia trachomatis, cryptosporidium, giardia lamblia, herpes simplex virus, human immunodeficiency virus, human papilloma virus, isospora belli, microsporisia, gonorrhea, viral hepatitis types B and C, and syphilis. Sexual transmission of some of these diseases is rare in the heterosexual population. Gays account for the lion's share of sexual-transmitted diseases not usually spread by sexual contact including hepatitis A, entamoeba histolytica,

Epstein-Barr virus, neisseria meningitides, shigellosis, salmonellosis, pediculosis, scabies and campylobacter.

There is clinical evidence that promiscuous people, in general, are more likely to be antisocial. As the gay sociologist Rotello reminds us: "...the outlaw aspect of gay sexual culture, its transgressiveness, is seen by many men as one of its greatest attributes." A 1995 study (Ellis et al.) found that 38% of homosexual men seeking treatment for urological problems had antisocial personality disorder, as contrasted with only 2% in the general population. The rate for prison inmates is 50%.

With such a high incidence of antisocial proclivities, it's no wonder that the gay community was quick to rummage through the Freudian literature in search of self-serving justifications for their inclinations. They argue that the unconscious mind is a repository of dark forces and it is best to bring them into consciousness and give them expression. And so it is that gay apologists began making claims for the therapeutic benefits of sadomasochism, preposterously calling it "a new dimension of love." The leather bars and fetish wear that are so prominent a feature of gay culture have little to do with love. It's all about dominance and submission, a resurgence of the master/slave dynamic. Clearly, the contemporary gay subculture is not a descendant of classical Greek homoerotism. The spiritual godfather of the modern gay scene is the Marquis de Sade.

To legitimize gay marriage would mean accepting this entire gay subculture into the American mainstream, which would not be good for the social health of our nation as a whole. In allowing gay marriage, the rest of society would, in effect, be marrying the homosexual counterculture. The gay community is eager to acquire the legitimacy that a marriage privilege would confer upon it, but gays don't want the scrutiny that the legislative process would bring. So much of what gays accept as commonplace in their subculture is repulsive to normal people. That's why homosexuals are thrilled that the gay social agenda is being imposed on American society by overreaching judges. The last thing gays want is a close examination of their behavior, their values, and their mental health. But such a detailed scrutiny is exactly what is needed in the gay marriage debate. Otherwise, straight America may wake up one morning to discover that it has become the Bride of Gay Frankenstein.

Chapter Eleven

Are Gays *Really* Just Like Black People?

The crown jewel of all the gay-activist arguments in favor of homosexual wedlock is the one that likens homosexuals to black people. According to gays, both blacks and gays share histories of exclusion and denigration; both blacks and gays have been denied their civil rights. The argument rounds itself out with a reminder that laws once prevented wedlock between blacks and whites and, by the same logic that led to the repeal of such laws, so must we now admit homosexual wedlock.

Needless to say, black folks, many of them deep-water Christians and Muslims, are not flattered by this comparison, nor should they be. Closer examination shows the comparison to be superficial and the argument to be without substance. To understand what makes the black and gay communities radically different requires a little history lesson. Please bear with me.

A Little History

Slavery in black Africa predated the arrival of the Europeans by millennia, so when some Dutchmen sitting in an Amsterdam coffeehouse hatched the idea for the triangular trade, they knew exactly where to go to buy slaves: Africa. They went to Africa because that's where the slave markets already existed. Their idea was to buy slaves in Africa, swap them for rum and molasses in the American tropics and then sell the rum and molasses for a profit in Europe. They would then spend their profits in the African slave markets and repeat this triangular trade route indefinitely.

The consequence of all this for white folks living in America was that they had few, if any, encounters with literate black people; the blacks they met seemed childlike, although some might display signs of cleverness and were deemed capable of God's redemption. These childlike qualities were used by slave masters to justify the institution of slavery. What they could not acknowledge was the power of the institution of slavery to stunt black intellectual development and make blacks *appear* to be the intellectual and moral inferiors of whites. What incentive does a slave have to be industrious, knowing that the fruits of his labors will be stolen from him? What decision-making capacity does someone have who has never been allowed to make his own decisions?

Long after emancipation the deforming influences of slavery, together with commonplace illiteracy and rustic rural manners, made many blacks socially repellent to white people and to sophisticated blacks as well. Only since the second half of the 20th Century have the great majority of black Americans been able to *demonstrate* their intellectual powers. The result has been the realization of Booker T. Washington's prediction that blacks would achieve social success as whites *witnessed* black achievement.

So what does all this have to do with the debate over gay marriage? Just this: we can follow the upward trajectory of black people's social status from their first encounter with Europeans to the present moment. Over that span of time blacks have retained a cultural distinctiveness while simultaneously becoming ever less alien. Contemporary blacks have far more in common with their white neighbors than with their illiterate animist ancestors, or even with African tribesmen today. They are modern Americans. As both races advanced and converged in social sophistication, the eugenic ordinances that were meant to protect society from the flaws of negritude came to seem quaintly antique. Somewhere along the way the lingering backwardness of some blacks became uncoupled from the idea of race and blacks became merely "the disadvantaged," in need of a job and some social skills.

In short, the notion of interracial marriage became less strange as the races ceased to be strangers. This form of exogamy is still far from commonplace because most people prefer the rhythms and shared assumptions of their home cultures, but black people, as a group, are no longer misidentified as the moral inferiors of any other racial group. The question before us now is the moral equivalency of blacks and homosexuals.

Why Gays Are Not the Moral Equivalent of Black People

The relationship of homosexuals to the greater society is not at all akin to the relationship of blacks to American society. The social histories of blacks and homosexuals are *wildly* different. The importation of African slaves was outlawed in 1808. In the 206 years since then, which is less than three human lifetimes laid end to end (70 years each), the social stock of American blacks has rocketed upward. Increased education and expanding opportunities have allowed blacks to demonstrate their intellectual and moral worth. The entire nation has been witness to this historic social wonder which even now continues its forward progress.

There is no such brightening perception of homosexuals. On the contrary, the more detailed information the average citizen is provided about contemporary homosexual **behavior**, the more alien homosexuals become. The social tolerance of gays has only gotten as far as it has because of a de facto "don't ask/don't tell" tradition among the well bred and the spin doctors of the liberal media. It's time to break that tradition and shine a white-hot spotlight on homosexual behavior; what we learn will illuminate the true essence of the homosexual psyche. Only then can each citizen make an **informed** opinion about the wisdom of folding the homosexual counterculture into mainstream American culture, elevating homosexual wedlock to the level of a sacrament, legitimizing homosexual behaviors, values and perspectives, and handing homosexuals the keys to every adoption agency in the land.

We should note in passing that homosexuality is not unitary. There are at least two homosexualities, and several sub-categories of each. The biological and social events that shape the homosexual mind are different for each sex and the results are distinctive. The norms of lesbian behavior and lesbian culture are very different from those of male homosexuals. Had they decided to go it alone, lesbians might have gained far more sympathy, but they have thrown in their lot with gay males, bisexuals and the transgendered, and so their destiny will depend on how much warmth the average person can gin up for anal erotics and surgically manufactured gender replicants. Homosexuals are a tiny fraction of the total population and lesbians are only about one third of that tiny fraction, so lesbians are a freakishly small percentage of the American population. In the arguments over homosexual wedlock it is the far larger and far more exotic population of male homosexuals who will shape the perception of homosexual wedlock in the public mind.

The Kinsey Institute study *Homosexualities*, which was published in 1978, revealed that nearly half of their white male homosexual sample reported *at least 500 different* sex partners, and this at an average age of 37 years. According to the Kinsey Institute, one third of gay men frequented bathhouses regularly and 62 percent sometimes used commercial settings for anonymous gay sex. The report confirmed that cruising, the hunt for sex with strangers, was a near universal habit of the gay male population. The authors did their best to put a happy face on these encounters by telling us that the gay sex seekers "spent at least several hours with their partners." Does this sound like a population that could make anything but a mockery of marriage? Now try to imagine what the moral status of the black population would be if a report revealed that the average black male had a sexual history of at least 500 women? Indeed, the *rising* social status of blacks has mirrored the *declining* perception of blacks as a promiscuous people. This perception was planted in the minds of many whites by the loose behavior and rustic manners of the waves of blacks who flooded northward after emancipation. No one was more shocked by these newcomers than were the long-acculturated and socially integrated northern blacks. Black newspaper editorials roundly denounced the loose morals of the newcomers. It was the natural human desire not to be near such randy and rustic people that led to the creation of the first urban ghettos for blacks, a phenomenon that had not existed in the North before that time. It was the birth of red-lining.

Given the history of black people and of their hard-won social status, the sudden demand for social acceptance by a notoriously promiscuous homosexual population strikes normal heterosexuals, white and black alike, as impudent counter jumping. Even the most sympathetic sociologists paint a bleak portrait of gay culture.

Land Humphreys was an Episcopal minister for ten years before becoming a graduate student in sociology in the 1960s. He devoted two years of his life to observing homosexual males sucking on each other's penises in public toilets. The homosexuals entered the toilets as strangers and performed sex acts on each other without uttering a word. Gays euphemistically call these toilets "tearooms." Humphreys' doctoral dissertation was later published under the title *The Tearoom Trade: Anonymous Sex in Public Places*.

Mr. Humphreys later said, "I have no moral or intellectual objection to what goes on in the "tearooms"... I do have a moral objection to the way in which society reacts to those who take part in that action." Humphreys had gone native; years later he would admit to being a homosexual himself. The notion of public decency doesn't seem to have entered his mind; the soulless vacancy of these encounters completely escaped his gay perception. Humphreys carried on his work in the hope of influencing public policy.

In conclusion, to equate the moral status of blacks with that of homosexuals is preposterous. The oppression of blacks began with a misapprehension of their true nature and was later sustained by the self-serving interests of slave owners. The primitive circumstances of slavery and Jim Crow delayed black development. Today, finally, we see the flowering of black potential. The convergence of the races, as both races became better educated and socially sophisticated, was to be expected. There is no *moral* disparity between the races.

Homosexuals, by contrast, are not even a genuine minority; they are not a race or a nationality; they are just a group of people with odd proclivities, anomalous perspectives, and the distinction of being considered mentally disordered by many mental health professionals. Homosexuals are held at arm's length because normal people find the intimate details of their behavior to be something somewhere between disturbed and disgusting. Homosexuals are unloved because of their **behavior**, which is repellent to millions of Americans.

Homosexuals are not the only anomalous humans to envision themselves as a victimized minority. Many deaf people now consider themselves to belong to a unique culture of the deaf. Their literature rails against the use of cochlear implants to give the sense of hearing to deaf children, an act that deaf militants liken to a kidnapping of one of their cultural tribesmen. Should society knuckle under to their demands and deny deaf children the gift of hearing?

And then there are the anorexics who argue that their shrunken bodies are an aesthetic choice, freely chosen, and that all attempts at intervention are a form of oppression. They have websites so they must be a real minority, right? Shouldn't we all just accept *their* vision of themselves as a minority and grant them their civil right to starve themselves?

The boldness of these special-interest groups is the organic consequence of the decades-long refinement of American identity politics: If you have a personal quirk, then make it the nucleus of your identity; after that unite with others who share your quirk and then declare yourselves to be a "minority" deserving of rights, recognition, political power and lots of taxpayer-funded benefits. That's the gay movement in a nutshell.

Bear in mind the explicit Kirk-and-Madsen gay agenda admonition to "Portray gays as *victims*." Gays want you to identify their discontents with genuine black tribulation. In short, homosexuals are trying to hop a free ride on the back of black oppression. Black folks aren't falling for it. Every public opinion poll demonstrates that the majority of black Americans are solidly against a homosexual marriage privilege.

Chapter Twelve

The Case Against One-Sex Wedlock

What Is Marriage?

In their bid to invent novel marriage modalities, gays are promoting the falsehood that marriage is just another lifestyle choice, a strictly personal matter created by the couple for themselves alone. This vision of marriage has a cozy romantic feel, but it paints an untrue portrait of marriage as a private affair between two people in which no one else, not even children of the couple, have or should have any interest. This same tunnel vision has been extended to include divorce, which is imagined to be nobody's business but the two wedded spouses.

The popular perception of marriage has already been cheapened by feminists who, since the 1970s, have denounced marriage as "slavery," and "legalized rape" in their headlong rush for personal autonomy and individual self-fulfillment. In 1962, 51 percent of women queried in a public opinion poll believed it was all right to dissolve a troubled marriage; by 1985 that number had leaped to 82 percent. To hell with the children, the fate of marriage now hung on a woman's perception of her personal happiness, a perception that feminists labored mightily to shape.

Once this cheapened notion of marriage as a strictly private matter got a toehold on the public imagination, marriage ceased to be thought of as an intensely important matter to children, and single motherhood took a giant leap upward in social status. In a 1993 *Los Angeles Times* article titled "Single Parent Issue Touches Sensitive Nerve," author Barbara Defoe Whitehead quotes an L.A. pastor as saying, "If a woman can't find Prince Charming and wants a baby and is ready, society should not dictate what is acceptable." What does he mean by "ready"? Does he mean rich like Rosie O'Donnell, or does he mean simply desirous of a baby? The trite and dismissive words "Prince Charming" to describe a mature man, a loyal husband and a loving father reveal the pastor's faint grasp of the importance of husbands, fathers and marriage. By the phrase "society should not dictate what is acceptable" this post-modern pastor is proclaiming his belief that society has no interest in the destruction of the institution of marriage, the elevation of single motherhood and the legion of fatherless *future* children who have never witnessed a healthy, sheltering and community-supported marriage of two mature adults – a husband and a wife. Perhaps it hasn't occurred to this pastor that the neighborhoods of South Central L.A. (ie, Compton) are now terrorized by twenty-five-year-old warlords and their armies of fatherless boys who look to them for the guidance and the male role-modeling that their out-of-wedlock moms were incapable of providing. Rogue males are the undoing of any civilized order and single motherhood is an incubator of rogue males. America's high crime rate is fueled by silly women making selfish reproductive decisions.

As more people come to imagine marriage to be merely an emotional relationship between two people, the bond of marriage comes to be seen as just one of many lifestyle choices, all of them equally honorable and of equal value. Following the lead of the radical feminists, homosexuals also pursued the demotion of marriage. As Gay Liberation became a movement for "gay rights" and homosexuals became more organized, gays became *political constituents* whose votes were eagerly sought by pandering politicians. Thereafter, cities and corporations, with the help of activist judges, began to extend the benefits of marriage to sundry couplings now deemed the "functional equivalent" of marriage. Soon the homosexuals were describing all special considerations to protect the institution of traditional marriage as "discrimination." The invention of "domestic-partnership" laws was nothing less than a government-sanctioned demotion of the institution of marriage; state and local governments had proclaimed that our civilization had no interest is supporting committed fathers and mothers.

The only reason that the male and female homosexual subcultures *exist* is because homosexuals sense the world *differently*. Gays have a psychological interior design all their own. To grant them a marriage privilege would be nothing less than the establishment of a radically new marriage paradigm, a mutant model of marriage, a *re-definition* of marriage so extreme as to define traditional marriage out of existence.

The first impulse of nice people is to want to be *nice*. We want to be friendly; we want to be *inclusive*. To all nice people I would say, "Your mother was right: Be cautious of strangers." The gay subculture is stranger than any "nice" person can imagine. To research this book I waded through thousands of pages of gay perspectives, gay imagery and gay pornography. Exploring the gay subculture can best be likened to touring a sewer in a glass-bottom boat.

Every father and mother model, as best they can, masculine and feminine virtue – the finest attributes of their genders. Men and women are acculturated differently, and in marriage one of us must accept and admire the different essence of the other. The emotional alchemy of this relationship and the intimate-stranger mystery that lies at its core is a daily presence in the life of every child who dwells in a traditional home. The subtle inflections of daily dad-and-mom dialog will form the background music of the next generation's intimate-stranger encounters with persons of their complementary gender. In short, parents are role-models for marriage; the future generation of normal parents will mimic the model of their normal parents.

Homosexuality, by contrast, is a house of mirrors. Homosexual couples are so alike in their essentials as to obliterate any hope of their ever successfully modeling the psychodynamics of normal heterosexual relationships. Any child trapped in a gay household has had the window of normal heterosexual perception slammed shut in his face. Two homosexuals are incapable of modeling the heterosexual social dynamic. The straight children of gay couples are gender expatriates raised in a foreign land of gay sensibility, surrounded by their parents' gay friends and awash in their parents' one-gender-only perspectives. Homosexuals are like the inhabitants of two-dimensional Flatland who struggle in vain to imagine a world of three dimensions – in this case, the world of normal heterosexuality. To put it bluntly, as models of romantic behavior and normal two-gender interaction, gay households are worse than useless.

Imagine a child reared in a normal two-parent home who for eighteen years was a witness to countless endearing, comical, stormy and sometimes perplexing, Mom-and-Dad interactions. For the child this collection of memories would be a deep reservoir of accumulated wisdom from which the child could draw future guidance. Now imagine how diminished this child would be if all those memories were erased. He or she would have taken a giant step backwards in social intelligence. Having a head full of memories of two gay dads is a pretty useless guide for young adults trying to navigate the foggy straits and coastlines of the *other* gender's psyche. You can't learn much about heterosexual interpersonal relations by observing homosexuals.

Chapter Thirteen

Experiments in Gay Marriage Go Haywire

Marriage is something larger than the feelings of two individuals; it is a unique institution rooted in custom, supported by law and respected by society. For most of the Twentieth Century marriage was so nearly universal as to be almost invisible. Couples married and raised families. Husbands supported their families; women specialized in the array of skills necessary to sustain a household in a time of few conveniences. Having children outside of wedlock was rare and disreputable.

Within a scant two generations all of this changed. The traditional order was done in by feminists, playboy philosophers, feel-good pop psychologists, welfare advocates and an ever-increasing tax burden that made one-wage-earner families a nostalgic memory. Hedonism, greed and the personal-fulfillment movement have all taken turns wounding the vital *social* institution of marriage. Marriage was demoted. The once clear distinction between holy wedlock and casual cohabitation became blurred. What was once understood to be a fundamental social institution came to be re-imagined as a private intimate relationship created by and for only two people for their own satisfaction. This vision is a sad remnant of what marriage should be and it's the common way in which homosexuals have spoken of marriage throughout the gay-marriage debate. Sadly, this demotion, this re-imagination of a fundamental institution, threatens the stability of American civilization. We can predict the future consequences of the privatization of marriage because others have already traveled this road to ruin.

Much to their detriment, Scandinavians went the gay-marriage route. In liberal Sweden and Denmark the citizens themselves embraced gay marriage; in more conservative Norway gay marriage was forced on an unwilling population be free-thinking judges and lawmakers. In each case the result was a catastrophe for children and the nurturing institution of marriage.

Because almost all gay marriages are childless, the very existence of gay marriage in Scandinavia enlarged the popular perception that marriage need not have anything to do with child rearing. In Norway, the overwhelmingly liberal media followed the gay-marriage debate closely and missed no opportunity to mock traditional Christian beliefs about the purposes of marriage and the responsibilities of mothers and fathers to their children. The Lutheran church had decried the growing trend of cohabitation and out-of-wedlock child bearing. These church traditionalists were derided by gays and the pro-gay clergy. When the dust had settled, the New Age theologians were in the saddle, extolling the virtues of a dawning Scandinavian gay utopia. And what was the consequence?

Today fully sixty percent of the children in Scandinavia are born out of wedlock. When the children are grown, most couples separate. A study by Yale University's William Eskridge in 2000 revealed that a mere 2,373 homosexual couples had chosen to marry in Denmark after a full nine years of acquiring the opportunity. After a full four years, only 749 gay couples had married in Sweden and a tiny 674 in Norway. When questioned about why so few homosexuals had actually married after creating so much social turmoil to acquire the privilege, the gays smugly replied that their argument that gay marriage would promote gay monogamy was just a cynical political tactic: their real goal "was not marriage but social approval for homosexuality."

We have every reason to believe that the American campaign for gay marriage is just as fraudulent and just as lacking in intellectual honesty as the three Scandinavian debates. The gays won in Scandinavia and the place is now a moral vacant lot with wall-to-wall out-of-wedlock children and a bloated socialist daycare system playing the role of absentee parents. Why would America want to fling its best life-sustaining institution into the gutter and follow Scandinavia down the ruinous gay-marriage rabbit hole?

For the damage that the cynical, self-serving gay community has done to the children of Scandinavia, the gay community deserves everyone's undying scorn. Likewise, by making a shambles of the greater social context that once supported marriage in Scandinavia, the gay community has once again demonstrated the destructive potential of its social perspectives. Thanks to their self-serving assault on tradition, marriage in Scandinavia is now virtually extinct. This disastrous large-scale Scandinavian experiment demonstrates exactly what will become of marriage in America if the gay social agenda gets any traction, and that includes the creation of any marriage-lite, commitment-lite, domestic-partnership-type civil unions.

The gay vision of marriage is a caricature of real marriage. Marriage is not a private affair; marriage transforms the human environment. Marriage creates a complex fabric of interwoven human obligations between the spouses and also between the larger society and every married person. For example, it is always morally wrong to participate in the breaking of a marriage vow, which is why all married people are always off limits to sexual opportunists and the emotionally needy.

Marriage is special because most marriages, predictably, produce offspring. The married couple is obligated to mold their offspring into healthy and responsible citizens. This two-decade-long obligation deserves the support of other social institutions for the long-term benefit of our civilization. Those unmarried people who see this consideration as an injustice against the unmarried are short sighted; they fail to see the support of marriage for what it is: one of society's long-term investments in its own preservation.

Even childless heterosexual couples support the institution of marriage by the traditional *form* of their marriages and the support they give to other married couples. That form is important because it maintains the social fabric of the traditional marriage culture. Wildly differing forms of marriage would only disrupt the marriage culture. Freakishly novel hybrid versions of marriage would enjoy little support from other marriages. If we are to judge from the Scandinavian disaster and the weak attraction to marriage by Canadian gays, there will never be enough gay marriages in America to form a mutually supporting network of gay marriages. At best, the collective of gay marriages will form an impoverished system of mutant marriages shunned by the traditional marriage culture because the anomalous role modeling of same-sex marriages makes the complicated enterprise of modeling marriage for the next generation of normal children even more complicated. Normal parents simply don't want to be burdened with the daily task of explaining away the strange deviations of the gay marriage microcosm. The legitimization of deviant models of marriage would be a distraction for normal parents who are struggling to raise the 99% of normal children who are the future parents of America.

No better example of the self-serving gay-marriage agenda can be found than the essay "Privatize Marriage: A Simple Solution to the Gay-Marriage Debate" by David Boaz, which first appeared in *Slate* on April 24, 1998 and has since been circulating as a collection of gay agenda talking points for the gay-marriage advocates in the liberal media. In his opening paragraph Boaz asks "...why should anyone have – or need to have – state sanction for a private relationship? As governments around the world contemplate the privatization of everything from electricity to Social Security, why not privatize that most personal and intimate of institutions, marriage?"

It's a very gay perspective. It's another attempt by a gay activist to narrow our attention down to just those two idiosyncratic individuals in a single relationship, thereby distracting us from the fact that marriage is a fundamental institution upon which entire civilizations depend. In America, the state governments act as gatekeepers to ensure that persons applying for a license to marry are people who, in fact, meet the minimal qualifications to enter into a marriage contract. For instance, the ability to understand the obligations of a marriage contract and to consent to those obligations is a *minimal* requirement to receive a license to marry. If the vital gate-keeping function were left to private persons (ie, the New Age clergy), then all sorts of quirky unions would crop up. The government declares that humans beneath the legal age of consent cannot enter into a marriage contract, no matter how much sadness this imposes on the hopeful homosexual boy-lovers at NAMBLA, so government oversight and licensing is a *good* thing;

the government is upholding the will of the people and the best interests our civilization.

In paragraph two Mr. Boaz tells us that privatization could mean removing the state completely from all matters relating to marriage. In other words, he doesn't want society, through the agency of society's elected representatives, to have any say in what constitutes a marriage in our society. Got that? Gays should be allowed to invent whatever sort of marriage arrangements give them pleasure; the rest of society should close its eyes and disregard any negative ripple effects that may emanate from these strange "marriages." The author generously adds that "Religious institutions are free to sanction such relationships under any rules they choose." Really? Our current immigration laws invite the Muslims of the world to join us here in America; their holy book approves of polygamy; it's one of the "rules they choose." Will polygamy be allowed? Or will society, through the agency of society's elected representatives, have a say in the matter?

Next, David Boaz suggests that the privatization of marriage could also mean that marriage is treated "like any other contract: The state may be called upon to enforce it, but the parties define the terms...the existence and details of such an agreement should be up to the parties." So..., if the contract calls for one of the marriage partners to be the leather-bound cabana-boy sex toy of the other partner, then the state should enforce the contract even as delicate Ramon pleads pitifully that he is worn out and only wants to flee the relationship and open a small antiques shop on Cape Cod? Not a chance.

Here's paragraph three: "And privatizing marriage would, incidentally, solve the gay marriage problem. It would put gay relationships on the same footing as straight ones, without implying official governmental sanction. No one's private life would have official government sanction – which is how it should be." This is the heart of the matter for homosexuals. They don't care at all about the long-term vitality of the institution of marriage; their first concern is to "put gay relationships on the same footing as straight ones." They hunger for respectability. Mr.

Boaz's fretfulness about "government sanction" is misplaced. The government is only a gatekeeper granting licenses to the qualified. It is society at large that will decide whether novel gay unions are nurtured or shunned.

Boaz ends with the snippy line, "…let's get the government out of marriage and allow individuals to make their own marriage contracts, as befits a secular, individualistic republic at the dawn of the information age." It's a very gay-male take on marriage. Mr. Boaz needs to be reminded that in our "secular" republic almost every marriage ceremony takes place in a religious context. In our "individualistic" republic marriage still represents the renunciation of the self-centered ethos of the individual in favor of a shared life for the greater good of both spouses and their children. The notion that this ancient and beneficial institution should undergo some sudden reevaluation "at the dawn of the information age" is a notion too gay for me to grasp. We have transistors; therefore we must also have gay marriage? I don't get it. Our technology and our vital social institutions are two distinctly different things.

The gay tactic here is to fragment the coherent community of mutually supporting heterosexual families. If marriage can be re-imagined as a cosmos of unique contractual agreements in which no human relationship is more life-enhancing or socially useful than any other, then even the most socially useless and degrading of human entanglements will be elevated to the honored status of a traditional husband-and-wife marriage.

Every culture has its unique ethos, its distinguishing mores, its fundamental values and spirit. The institution of marriage is an organic expression of the complementary nature of the heterosexual relationship. Each complementary couple, bonded in marriage, becomes a living organ of the much larger organism that is the marriage culture, the culture of bonded couples. Each couple, in principle, becomes the nucleus of a possible family. The community of families forms the nursery of the nation. It is here that the young learn life-sustaining lessons about normal human bonding and normal gender deportment. Those couples who do not form families still strengthen the marriage culture, so long as they model normal pair-bonding behavior.

Couples from subcultures that do not model normal pair bonding are the organs of an alien organism. The most outstanding contribution of homosexuals to the marriage culture would be confusion. Everyone knows this; it's the reason why proponents of gay marriage try to shape the issue as a matter of individual liberty, as a matter of "gay rights." By narrowly focusing attention on gay *individuals*, they distract us from the negative consequences a homosexual ethos would have on any host culture. Gay men are notoriously promiscuous. With an average personal history of hundreds of different, mostly anonymous, sexual encounters the only heterosexuals to rival gays are professional sex-trade workers and a few celebrities. Does anyone believe that married gay males will suddenly forget the way to Fire Island or the nearest bathhouse? To quote Andrew Sullivan, "Many gay men value this sexual freedom more than the stresses and strains of monogamous marriage (and I don't blame them)." I will have more to say about Andrew Sullivan later.

The Gay Marriage Trojan Horse

The most frequent defense of gay marriage is presented in the form of a question. It usually goes something like this, "What possible harm would result if dear old Bert and Ernie got married?" A variation of this argument is, "What harm would come to your traditional marriage if homosexuals were free to marry one another?" These are not really arguments at all; they are a challenge to heterosexuals to produce arguments in defense of traditional wedlock. This is backwards; the burden is on the gay challengers to convince society that gay marriage would do no harm to existing institutions.

Take note that gay arguments are usually atomistic. Questions about Bert & Ernie or "your marriage" are meant to focus your attention on the microcosm of one gay couple or just *your* marriage, and to turn your attention away from the bigger question:

111

Would the creation of a gay marriage privilege weaken America's social fabric and diminish the utility of its sustaining institutions?

Asking you what possible harm one gay marriage would cause is like asking a pathologist what possible harm one bacterium would cause. The answer is, probably no harm at all. The host would cope with one bacterium. But what about ten bacteria? Or a million? Using this analogy we are moved to wonder, "Would commonplace gay marriages produce social pathologies?" And, "Would gay marriage weaken vital social institutions?" Is gay marriage a Trojan Horse best left outside the fortress of our traditional marriage culture? There are reasons to believe that it is.

When asked how gay marriage would harm *your* marriage, the best answer may be that it would harm your marriage by screwing up and rendering untrustworthy a network of social institutions that now support and protect the traditional marriage culture. By granting gays a marriage privilege our traditional culture would, in effect, be entering into a marriage with the homosexual counterculture. Allowing gays to marry one another, solemnizing their anomalous unions, is nothing less than legitimizing homosexuality and homosexual perspectives. The gay community is well aware of this subtext to the gay marriage debate; that's why gays who personally shun monogamy are still eager to realize a gay marriage privilege. The legitimacy that a marriage privilege would confer upon gays is their passport into the most intimate inner sanctums of our social institutions. To grasp the implications of what this would mean we should examine a few social institutions where pockets of gay culture have gained a toehold.

A Cancer on the Catholic Church

The Catholic Church is presently undergoing a gut wrenching self-appraisal. The tragedy of widespread sexual molestations and rapes by Catholic priests, spanning decades, has its roots in one tragic oversight: the Church allowed a homosexual culture to establish itself within the Catholic seminary schools. By the latest accounting, about 4% of American Catholic priests have been implicated in sexual improprieties. This is probably an undercount.

112

The molestation of boys and young men is wildly underreported. Those homosexual priests who have done no wrong, nonetheless, by their very presence, enlarged the gay comfort zone within the Church. Any gay enclave is a self-reinforcing engine of promiscuous gay permissiveness.

There has been much loose talk about "pedophile priests," probably because this alliteration trips off the tongue so nicely. But an examination of the Church's report on the sex scandals shows scant signs of pedophilia. Pedophilia is a sexual attraction to *pre-pubescent* humans. Puberty in our era usually starts at age eleven years; it's all over by age thirteen. Gay sex with post-pubescent boys is called pederasty, not pedophilia, and it is just another form of homosexuality. Pederasts are just plain homosexuals. So, in truth, the Catholic Church has a problem caused by indwelling pockets of homosexual culture that are inimical to the Church's Christian mission.

On February 28, 2004 the *Newark Star Ledger* published the results of a national survey commissioned by the U.S. Conference of Catholic Bishops to determine the extent and nature of sexual abuse by its clergy, based on an analysis of abuse reports from 1950 to 2002. According to this report 81 percent of the victims were male. Only 22%, about one-fifth, could be classified as pedophilia. Fully 78% of the reported sexual indecencies were victimizations of youths between the ages of 11 and 17 years. The report illustrated how the percentage of homosexual victimizations steadily increased over time from 64% in the 1950s to 76% in the 1960s, to 86% in the 1970s. It remained at the 86% level through the 1980s; there is no information included for later years. Especially telling is the single line under the heading "Accused priests who also have been abused, by type of abuse," which reads "Sexual abuse – 65%". This tells us that homosexual contact is especially damaging to the normal development of a healthy male psyche. According to the report 28% of the abuses involved clothing being stripped from the victim; 27% involved a homosexual sucking on the victim's penis, and in a quarter of the cases the abuser attempted or achieved full penile penetration of the victim.

Sister Mary Ann Walsh, spokeswoman for the U.S. Conference of Catholic Bishops, echoed the view of several sociologists when she observed that the number of abuse claims, 10,669, under-represents the size of the victim population. Some experts estimate that the victim population might be as large as 100,000. To quote the *Newark Star Ledger*: "Though the study did not blame celibacy or homosexuality for the abuse, it said better understanding of each, and acknowledgment of 'significant changes in sexual behavior in the culture at large' in the 1960s and 1970s, were required to properly understand the crisis." This is nothing but coy "clergy-speak." The "significant changes in sexual behavior" alluded to were the collapse of traditional societal restraints on sexual promiscuity and the Jack-in-the-Box eruption of its dark companion, Gay Liberation, with all its half-baked rationalizations for why homosexuals deserve entrée to the deepest recesses of our social institutions: our churches, our schools, our youth organizations, our military barracks and the very cornerstone institution of our culture, marriage.

Quoting the Conference of Catholic Bishops: "In some instances, according to one bishop, the culture of, 'If it feels good, it's all right' infiltrated seminaries...As a result, a homoerotic culture took root at some seminaries" and a "'gay subculture' developed." And further, "The Board was told that some seminarians were propositioned (or worse) by older seminarians or faculty, and little was done when complaints were made about this misconduct." In other words, homosexuals had colonized the Catholic seminaries and young seminarians were being victimized by the homosexual colonizers.

Seminary candidates were not asked their sexual orientation until the 1990s. Today, a sadder-but-wiser Church asks this question routinely. The investigators approve, saying that "a more searching inquiry is necessary for a homosexually oriented man by those who decide whether he is suitable for the seminary and for ministry." It's amazing to watch so-called "smart people" using research committees to acquire the common sense of the average American. Any normal twelve-year-old boy could tell any social service provider to "hold back the homosexuals."

114

The Suffering That Gays Cause

On March 8th, 2004, the *Newark Star Ledger* featured an article titled "Support builds for abuse victims" and subtitled "More males seeking help in group sessions." The first line of staff writer Ana Alaya's inquiry reads: "Mark Goebel says he was twelve the first time the 'monster' raped him." Ms. Alaya goes on to detail Mark's two-year ordeal at the hands of a homosexual teacher at a boarding school in Princeton, NJ. Said Mr. Goebel, "I didn't even know how to share an experience like that with someone, how to get beyond the fear, the flashbacks, especially when I was hoping to put myself in a loving sexual relationship with another person."

The tragic consequences of the colonization of Catholic Church institutions by homosexuals have brought the subject of toxic gay contact into the spotlight. "The recent exposure has begun to break the isolation," says Mark Crawford, a board member of the national group Male-Survivor, a support group for male victims of sexual abuse. In Bergen County, NJ, inquiries from male victims to the YMCA's Rape Crisis Center have doubled. A new support group for male victims has attracted more than thirty men. The Essex County Rape Crisis Center is also inaugurating a program for male victims of homosexuals. The director, Ursula Liebowitz, said, "I firmly believe male victims are forgotten victims. They feel the rape crisis centers are a women's world."

The Saint Luke's Roosevelt Hospital in New York has added a second group therapy session to its Crime Victim's Treatment Center. Louise Kindley, a social worker at the Victim's Center said that more male victims have been encouraged to come forward because of the clergy scandal. "A lot of men I see are coming from AA, Debtors Anonymous and other groups. I think more people are talking about the abuse in the 12-step rooms. It's a very big change, and a good change," Kindley explained.

The Survivors Network for those Abused by Priests (SNAP) has grown dramatically from two chapters in 2002 to 57 chapters today. This group has 5,000 members, some of whom were abused by homosexuals other than clergy.

At a SNAP meeting in Mendham, NJ, Bob Deacon revealed how his life was "disrupted" for 40 years by suicide attempts and ruined relationships because a homosexual abused him when he was young. Mr. Deacon explained, "I'm shedding the guilt and the shame." Mark Goebel said his abuse at the hands of a homosexual teacher at the American Boychoir School nearly ruined his life. He drank heavily throughout college and military service and was constantly on guard to contain his "combustible anger." The teacher was dismissed after two other students reported the teacher's sexual advances toward them.

According to a widely quoted study by David Finkelhor, a sociology professor at the University of New Hampshire, one of every six boys is the victim of sexual abuse before they reach the age of eighteen years. Both male and female victims of sexual exploitation experience shame and guilt, but experts point out that male victims carry additional burdens. Richard Gartner is the author of *Betrayed as Boys: Psychodynamic Treatment of Sexually Abused Men*. Mr. Gartner explained, "To acknowledge yourself as a victim means to many boys that they are not male and that stops them from talking to other men about it. Intertwined with that can be confusion about sexuality, if the boy is abused by a man."

Exactly! Sexual contact with homosexuals is **especially** damaging to the healthy emotional development of young males: it creates self-doubt; it diminishes self-worth; it deepens confusion in an already confused young person. It can also foster rage and embitterment and, in some cases, a pathological desire to reverse roles with the victimizer by *becoming* a victimizer. Remember: 65% of the accused Catholic priests said that they themselves had been the victims of early sexual abuse. So the toxic touch of a homosexual predator can reach out across generations. All the men whose bright futures were derailed by contact with homosexuals were on a journey to become emotionally healthy husbands and have fulfilling marriages and model healthy manhood for their children. For many of them this is a shattered dream. To those who wonder aloud how gay marriage would harm the marriages of heterosexuals, I answer that **any** homosexual infiltration into any institution that is intended to be an incubator of healthy manhood

116

is a menace to the future marriages of normal heterosexuals. America needs healthy husbands, and healthy fathers and healthy marriages rooted in healthy heterosexual relationships. Anything that encourages the growth of the gay subculture is a menace to healthy heterosexual development.

Chapter Fourteen

Answering Andrew Sullivan

Collectively, the arguments for mainstreaming the homosexual counterculture are no more than a grab-bag of unsubstantiated speculations about how the radical gay social agenda will be good for American civilization. In the arena of ideas, certain gay gladiators have gained a reputation as the ones to beat in the gay marriage debate. I have considered their best arguments; I am not impressed. The most distinguished advocate of gay marriage is Andrew Sullivan; gays seem to think that Andrew is the "go-to" guy for a snappy defense of homosexual wedlock. As a gay advocate, Mr. Sullivan has won acclaim as the gay Left's favorite torpedo in their current assault on traditional social values.

On February 16, 2004, *Time* magazine published Mr. Sullivan's plea for gay marriage titled "Why the 'M' Word Matters to Me." It's an embarrassing revelation written in the earnest "How I Spent My Summer Vacation" style so dear to fifth graders. Its opening line reads, "As a child, I had no idea what homosexuality was." For little Andrew, his life was all downhill from there.

Andrew tells us that he "grew up in a traditional home." That's where he learned that "The most important day of your life was when you got married," which is *so gay*. I too grew up in a traditional home and neither I, nor any of my normal male friends, *ever* gave a moment's thought to the day when we might escort a bride to an altar. We were **guys**, not gays. Fretting about that "most important day" never entered our heads. Marriage was for grown-ups, for parents and grandparents and aunts and uncles and other remnants of the Age of Dinosaurs.

Andrew reveals to us that as he grew older "I didn't feel the things for girls that my peers did. All the emotions and special rituals and bonding of teenage heterosexual life eluded me." Andrew was becoming aware of his in-dwelling quasi-autistic inability to respond to the half of humanity who are every normal man's gender complement. Young Andrew grew confused: "My emotional bonds to other boys were one-sided; each time I felt myself falling in love, they sensed it, pushed it away."

Of *course* they pushed it away! Ninety-nine percent of boys have a biological destiny that is distinct from that of a homosexual. The budding oddness of gayness will only elicit discomfort from normal boys.

Andy immersed himself in schoolwork, "anything to give an excuse not to confront reality," as he put it. Andy frets, "Would I ever have the most important day of my life?" He imagines that if only he can manage a marriage he will, at last, become a "full part" of his family, as if marriage, like a new garment, will make him, somehow, more normal. The thought that his homosexual marriage might shock and revolt his "Catholic, conservative, middle class" family never enters his clueless gay head.

Andrew Sullivan reveals that "like many teens, I withdrew, became neurotic, depressed, at times close to suicidal." This gay intellectual wants us to believe that his teenage angst is typical of gay teens and that his gayness was the sole cause of his malaise. To put this in perspective, fully 15% of humanity is afflicted with a genetically-based predisposition to shyness. These people feel ill at ease in social situations – always. There are about fifteen times as many shy people as there are gays. So shyness causes about fifteen times more instances of social isolation as does gayness, but we are asked to feel some special sympathy for gays. Why? Why aren't shy people as worthy of our sympathy as homosexuals?

Mr. Sullivan's real purpose is to exploit his unhappy adolescence for political advantage. He has suffered the pangs of unrequited love from his male friends; therefore society owes Andy the institution of gay marriage. It's a sad old song: Nobody knows the trouble he's seen. But ask yourself, would any parent want young Andy Sullivan putting the moves on *their* son? Not a chance. Andy was born with strange proclivities; therefore Andy is destined to live the life of a marginal person. Andrew Sullivan longs to be celebrated on his "most special day," but most people find the celebration of any relationship rooted in an abnormality to be a bit creepy, at best.

Gay relationships are in some other category; they are a striking deviation from normal behavior; they are a flagrant repudiation of the complementary "other;" they are a rejection of the central dynamic of traditional marriage. Any barrier that exists between Mr. Sullivan and his family is one created by Mr. Sullivan's own exceptional sexual appetites.

Were Andy's mom and dad hoping to have a warm relationship with Andy's future wife? Would they be just as thrilled sharing the holidays with Andy's husband, or male bride, or whatever? Andy might think so because Andy is lost in Gay Fantasy Land, a theme park of the mind where gays have convinced themselves that merely acquiring the external trappings of heterosexual courtship will magically win them social acceptance.

Andrew Sullivan would have us believe that just because consensual gay sex acts between adults in private are no longer illegal in the United States, we should embrace gays as people who are "just like us." It's a sly argument that attempts to gloss over the meaningful distinction between what is merely legal and what is *legitimate*, what is proper, and what is in the best interest of a healthy and robust social order. Is there any part of the gay counterculture that can be described as the cornerstone of a robust society? Gay society is a self-indulgent biological dead end punctuated here and there by a few relationships that include children, most of whom were transported from previous relationships in which the homosexual defrauded a normal heterosexual into believing that the homosexual was a normal human.

Declaring the strange behaviors of homosexuals to be legal does not render them any less strange. Legality is the bare minimum that society demands of its members. The decriminalization of what gays do in private is a measure of society's tolerance; it is not a measure of society's acceptance of gay behavior.

Andrew Sullivan goes on to suggest that the quest for gay marriage is a campaign for greater familial responsibility by gays. That's laughable. Does anyone honestly believe that a child who grew up

121

in the Castro district of San Francisco, who was dragged to every gay pride parade, who summered with gays on Fire Island, who was always surrounded by mom's lesbian pals or daddy's effeminate boyfriends will ever witness enough **normal** adult heterosexual interaction to ever become the sort of person whom our culture would define as a healthy man or woman? Every normal child held captive in the gay subculture lives a life of heterosexual-culture malnutrition. Because homosexuals are neither men nor women, they are incapable of modeling genuine masculine or feminine virtue. Gays are simply gays. They can only model the gayness that is their essence.

It is in the interest of society to strengthen every heterosexual union and to encourage marriage as the best context for childrearing. Society has no similar interest in encouraging gay relationships. A child must be exposed to *both* gender models, both of them interacting over a span of years, before the child can understand how these two *complementary* role models coexist and harmonize. This is how children pick up the beat, the happy rhythm, of normal male/female interaction. Deviant models of human interaction can only model deviance. Because heterosexuals outnumber gays by almost one hundred to one, a gay parent with a child will almost certainly have a *heterosexual* child, for whom the gay parent can only model inappropriate gender behavior. Bringing an occasional friend or relation into the child's life to "model" the missing gender dimension simply makes a mockery of the importance of the missing mother or father. As far as children are concerned, gay marriage is a cruel hoax. These kids may grow up to be heterosexual, but they will be inept heterosexuals. They are the kids who learned heterosexuality as a "second language."

Homosexuals are now a political constituency of the Democratic Party and for that reason alone taxpayers must bankroll lavish drug programs to assist gays with their self-inflicted diseases and we *must* support gay marriage because gays want it and will stomp their feet and threaten to withhold donations from Democrat politicians if the Democrat politicians fail to deliver the goodies.

With that said, we should note that enthusiasm for gay marriage is far from unanimous among gays themselves. Many gays would be pleased to see the whole gay-marriage parade float go up in flames. In the September 1996 issue of *Details*, gay writer John Weir disapproved of gay marriage, insisting that gayness was a critical posture against bourgeois convention: "I thought the whole point of being homosexual was to poke fun at heterosexual convention. When you commit yourself to being gay you're supposed to take a lifelong vow of otherness. You're supposed to live on the outside, to glory in being different." But Andy Sullivan doesn't want to be the "permanent Other" no matter how deeply the gay counterculture has taken a "lifelong vow of otherness." The gay community, it seems, has a split personality on matters such as monogamy, fidelity and all that other stuff that is traditional to heterosexual culture.

Chapter Fifteen

Deflating Gay Fantasies

If you enter the words "gay" and "domestic violence" in the Google search engine you will instantly get 219,000 website descriptions, most of them public-service sites created by gays themselves. It's convincing evidence that partner abuse and violence are epidemic among gays and lesbians. At the www.lambda.org website the title reads "Domestic Violence Prevalent in Lesbian, Gay, Bisexual and Transgender Relationships." We are told that "Between 25% and 33% of relationships between lesbian, gay, bisexual, or transgender partners include abuse…" Statistics compiled by the National Coalition of Anti-Violence Programs documented 3,327 cases in 1997, which was a 41% increase (975) over the previous year. The number of abuse reports by gays (52%) and lesbians (48%) were essentially equal. They concluded that gay-community violence "appears to be vastly under-reported."

The truth blows a big hole in the myth that gay, and especially lesbian, relationships exist on some higher moral plane than man/woman relationships. An article in the *Calgary Sun* (3/19/04), titled "Gay Abuse in Shadows" gives the view from Canada: "The happy-go-lucky gay lifestyle often portrayed by the media often comes with a dark side of mental, physical, and sexual abuse, said a crisis counselor. Jane Oxenbury, a psychologist with Edan Counseling Associates in Calgary, said research shows close to 33% of people in homosexual relationships are in fact being abused."

A National Institutes of Health study appeared in December 2002; it revealed that HIV-positive males were more likely to be the targets of gay violence: "Perhaps the most startling and disturbing finding was that being HIV-positive increases the likelihood of being physically battered," said Reif. "Many men in the study were subjected to physical and emotional violence after telling their partners they had been diagnosed with HIV. Tragically, men who rely on abusive partners for financial support often are forced to make the impossible choice between violence and homelessness." How's that for sensitivity?

From England, Dr. Stephen Eccles, a clinical psychologist at the Manchester Mental Health Partnership, tells us: "Additional forms of abuse may occur which are unique to same-sex partnerships, such as threatening to out a partner to family and friends." Other examples include coercing partners by threatening to reveal their HIV status. Dee Shelly of the educational charity Gay and Lesbian Arts and Media (GLAM) in Brighton says there is a conspiracy of silence in the gay community: "It's like washing our dirty linen in public. We don't want straight people thinking we're just as bad as they are. With lesbians, the idea is that we're all feminist, loving women who don't do that 'male stuff.' But it's bullshit – a woman is as likely to thump her partner as a man. And gay men don't want to be seen as victims." So the lesbians are in deep denial that their ranks include lots of hard-knuckled control freaks and the gays don't want to be seen as effeminate pushovers, and all of them want to deceive the normal world into believing that gay relationships are the last best hope for reviving the sick-and-dying institution of marriage.

Mr. Carpenter's assertion that "instances" of infidelity will occur in gay marriages is too laughable to countenance. The only heterosexuals who even approach the average gay for promiscuity are professional sex workers. To suggest that gay marriages would suddenly become models of monogamous probity is ridiculous. Gay marriages will be a reflection of the gay culture; they will be queer parodies of traditional marriage. These parodies can only diminish public esteem for the institution of marriage. The infiltration and colonization of the institution of marriage by homosexuals will prove every bit as damaging as their colonization of Catholic institutions.

The March 12th, 1998 issue of the *Windy City Times* included "Gay Marriage: Ready, Set..." by gay author Paul Varnell, in which he cautions the many gays who eagerly anticipate that a gay marriage privilege will magically stabilize their shaky gay relationships. He says that gay "couples may choose to marry hoping that legal structure will solidify an unstable and uncertain relationship. But many of those will find, as heterosexual couples have found for centuries, that marriage is not a panacea, that it does not improve the other person, (in fact often the opposite)..."

The very existence of a gay marriage privilege will put new pressure on *all* gay relationships. As Paul Varnell observes, "...couples may feel that their relationship is fine the way it is and decide not to marry. But that in itself will look like a statement about the relationship since they are not taking the next available step. That is, relationships that previously looked and felt fully 'committed,' now if not legalized may seem 'not fully committed,' even 'keeping our options open' without any inherent change in the relationship. Family and friends will wonder if the couple really is committed – even if the couple really is [a couple]."

As Paul Varnell says, all gays would be subject to "encouragement by friends, relatives and other gay couples to 'settle down,' 'tie the knot,' and so forth, when marriage becomes available...Every culture or society, after all, tends to develop favored forms of behavior, certain ways they expect people to behave, forms that are believed to conduce to the social benefit." Well, yes. That's why gays are considered queer rogues, but Varnell's point is that gays would be *expected* to marry if gay marriage were legal. The noisy campaign to legalize gay marriage would legitimize efforts by the straight majority to pressure gays to marry and quit the gay counterculture's favorite bastions of anonymous gay sex: the bathhouses, the "tea rooms," the public parks, the summer rentals on Fire Island, etc.

Says Varnell, "...the fact that you will be able to marry will now linger in the back of your mind when you go home with someone for sex, when you go on a date, when you start 'seeing' someone. The fact that you could actually marry this person means you will be asking yourself if you really would want to, and that may subtly encourage many of us to take our casual relationships with other gays a little more seriously..."

Because gay marriage would have serious consequences for mainstream society, it will also have serious consequences for the gay counterculture. The first consequence is that the gay world must cease to be a counterculture. Otherwise, gay marriage will have nothing but toxic consequences for marriage itself. In short, a gay marriage privilege is a license for mainstream heterosexual society to radically remodel the gay subculture. It would be a stunning makeover for the queer folk, a sort of *Clear Eye for the Queer Guy*, with a vengeance. The next port of call for the gay Love Boat will be radical domestication.

Paul Varnell says that "If the law stipulates that our relationships are the legal equivalent of theirs, that will be considerable encouragement for them to begin thinking of us and our lives as equal to them and their lives." Not exactly. Before straights could even "begin thinking" of gays as equal to themselves, the gays would have to begin *behaving* like straight people. The depravity of gay promiscuity must be buried in the Boot Hill of bad behaviors before straights can "begin thinking" of gays as their moral equals.

Then Paul Varnell serves up this amazing gay confection: "Many heterosexuals have in the back of their minds, and some are still brought up to believe, the notion that a marriage certificate basically says, 'Sex is OK now.' So when gay men start getting marriage certificates, people are going to see the law as asserting not only the equality of our relationships, but an equal status and dignity for our sexual behavior. And that, for many people will be a remarkable and startling thought."

Yes, indeed, it will. What Paul is suggesting is that the legalization of gay marriage will also bring with it a dearly sought legitimization of homosexual behaviors, "an equal status and dignity for our [gay] behavior." Paul is much too clever a propagandist to ever *specify* the exact behaviors that would attain "equal status and dignity," so Paul won't be extolling the dignity of full blown anal intercourse, complete with anal lacerations, or the dignity of cramming his fist up another guy's rectum, or the elevated stature of licking some guy's anus (anilingus), or the

128

proud tradition of urinating in your partner's face and mouth (golden showers), not to mention the catalog of time-honored sexual behaviors bequeathed to the gay community by the Marquis de Sade.

Almost every expression of gay sexuality strikes normal folks as an affront to human dignity. Only by using bland expressions such as "gay sex" can homosexuals hope to advance their social agenda. Only by cloaking their behaviors in euphemism can gays promote homosexual wedlock.

Paul Varnell understands that "religious conservatives" will "loathe" the legitimization of popular homosexual behaviors. Says Varnell, "They feel that if you cannot maintain that homosexual acts are wrong, then you cannot claim that anything at all is wrong, 'everything is permitted,' and moral chaos will reign…" Well . . . sort of. The reason conservatives believe that these homosexual acts are "wrong" is because they are also degrading. Would a loving husband urinate in his wife's face? Even the homosexuals of ancient Greece refused to be the recipients of anal intercourse; they would have considered modern gays debased and deplorably effeminate, the pathetic torchbearers of a slave ethos. What sane person wants to contaminate his expressions of love with excrement? What makes gays so profoundly alien to others is their habituation to deviant appetites totally lacking in simple human dignity. Proper toilet training should have closed the door on most gay sexual behavior. Nonetheless, gays from coast to coast now want us to grant them the respect usually reserved for a bride in white.

Chapter Sixteen

A Few Words About Polygamy

Paul Varnell's essay "Gay Marriage, then Polygamy?" was published in the *Chicago Free Press* on February 25, 2004. It's a goldmine of gay nonsense. The author opens by saying that "When some opponents of gay marriage try to argue for their view, after they ritually condemn homosexuality they claim that gay marriage 'damages society' and 'undermines marriage' in some unspecified way and end by postulating deplorable consequences of gay marriage: 'If we allow gay marriage, then people will want to practice polygamy and marry their pets'."

Well, there is nothing ritualistic or unspecific about the arguments against gay marriage that I have presented to you. Varnell really wants to convey the notion that opponents of gay marriage do not have reasoned arguments to present, which is untrue. The line about pets is a nonstarter. Pets can't marry because pets can't *consent* to a marriage contract. People toss that line into the debate simply to illustrate that mutual affection is insufficient to support a claim to a right to marry. The issue of polygamy can't be dismissed so lightly.

The Question of Polygamy

There are thousands of practicing polygamists in North America and vastly more in the larger world. Had polygamists been the first to petition for a right to legalize polygamy, the first argument against them would have been that if polygamy were legalized there would soon be a movement to legalize gay marriage. The fact that gays are presenting their petition first is just an accident of history. If American society were compelled to choose between the legalization of polygamy or gay marriage, then polygamy, with its familiar central male/female dynamic, would probably be preferred. Far and away, polygamy would be understood to be the more socially useful of the two social arrangements. At the very least, polygamists can claim to have met society's definitions of

131

what it means to *be* a woman and to *be* a man, while gays and lesbians leave us quizzical.

There are millions of Muslims in America. Their holy book approves of responsible polygamy. American law, which is rooted in Western Christian culture, prohibits polygamy because it offends *our* cultural sensibilities. By contrast, **no** holy book approves of homosexuality; it is roundly condemned with every mention. The laws prohibiting consensual gay sex are rooted in our time-honored customs. These laws were voided by the *Lawrence vs. Texas* decision even though the particulars of gay sex continue to offend the public's moral sensibility. The implications of this were not lost on Justice Antonin Scalia. Referring to the case of *Bowers vs. Hardwick* which had upheld Georgia laws against homosexual sodomy, Justice Scalia wrote in his dissenting opinion in *Lawrence vs. Texas* that "State laws against bigamy, same-sex marriage, adult incest, prostitution, masturbation, adultery, fornication, bestiality, and obscenity are likewise sustainable only in light of moral choices. Every single one of these laws is called into question by today's decision; the Court makes no effort to cabin the scope of its decision to exclude them from its holding. The impossibility of distinguishing homosexuality from other traditional 'morals' offenses is precisely why Bowers rejected the rational-basis challenge. 'The law,' it said, 'is constantly based on notions of morality and if all laws representing essentially moral choices are to be invalidated under the Due Process Clause, the courts will be very busy indeed.'

"What a massive disruption of the current social order, therefore, the overturning of Bowers entails..."

But overturn Bowers they did; by judicial fiat they discarded the moral wisdom of thousands of years of human experience. If the moral sensibilities of the people of a culture are no longer the foundation of their laws, then any offensive behavior that does not cause physical injury can be defended as someone's "right." So how can American society now defend itself against polygamy, which is an accepted practice under Islamic law? How many Mormons are biding their time as the gay-marriage debate grinds

132

on? In the towns of Colorado City and Hildale, Arizona, there are about 7,500 residents who comprise one large polygamous enclave, where nearly every man has more than one wife and sometimes dozens of children. The Mormon Church officially renounced polygamy in 1890 and the practice is forbidden by a Utah state law, which is only sporadically enforced.

On what grounds could the courts now grant "sodomites" a marriage privilege while denying an expanded marriage privilege to righteous Mormons and Muslims and immigrants from those African nations where polygamy is a time-honored tradition? What about the "dignity" of *their* relationships, to echo the words Justice William Renquist used in his *Lawrence* decision.

Once Americans have acquired the newfangled "right" to homosexual wedlock *and* polygamy, can gay polygamy be far behind? Imagine it: twenty lesbians all married to a twenty-first lesbian. Would they all troop to the sperm bank together? Would there be schoolbooks with titles such as "Heather Has Twenty Mommies"? Would sex within the family be restricted to lovemaking between Lesbian Number One and her satellite lesbians or would they all have romps with each other? In heterosexual polygamy, sex between the wives is not a part of the normal dynamic. In gay polygamy the usual gay longings would undermine all restraint. So, would intra-family sex without Lesbian Number One be considered marital infidelity, since the satellite lesbians aren't married to each other? Tradition couldn't guide us here; we'd be lost in the confusion of Gay Utopia and all because we allowed our culture to be colonized by homosexuals with alien moral perspectives.

For extra credit, try to imagine a polygamous family of gay males. Viagra, everyone? While you're at it, imagine a criminal gang of straight males who intermarry to obtain a spousal protection against compelled testimony. Law enforcement would be frustrated because the thugs were married to their gang leader. There's no end to how weird our republic could become.

Paul Varnell asserts that "Gays are not arguing that people should be able to have whatever marital arrangement they want. They argue only that everyone should have access to marriage as it is now commonly understood. Nor are gays arguing for any legal rights other people do not have. They argue that they are uniquely denied a right everyone else already has – the right to marry someone they love." The truth is that the *Lawrence* decision, which gays celebrate, has undermined the foundation of *all* morals legislation, including the laws against bigamy, polygamy and incest. Furthermore, Varnell's statement that gays are only arguing that everyone should have access to marriage as it is now commonly understood is nonsense. Everyone *does* have access to marriage as it is commonly understood. Any adult male can now enter into a consensual marriage with an adult female and any adult female can enter into a consensual marriage with an adult male, therefore **everyone** now has equal access to marriage as it is commonly understood. Most gays (not all) choose to **not** exercise their right to marry. As years of accumulated evidence attest, gays in Canada, Europe and Scandinavia overwhelmingly choose to **not** exercise their privilege to gay marriage when it is offered to them. What gay activists in America are *really* arguing for are completely new social institutions to which they want to attach the name marriage, even though these novel institutions would only ape traditional marriage in a coarse parody; the essential male/female dynamic that is the essence of traditional heterosexual marriage would be forever absent.

Paul Varnell believes that "It is hard to imagine many women in the contemporary U.S. cheerfully welcoming competing wives or voluntarily becoming a second, third, or fourth wife." He should get out of his urban gay bubble more often; not all of America is like Manhattan or San Francisco. The wives in a wisely composed polygamous family do not compete, they cooperate harmoniously; they share the burden of maintaining a well-run household; they are companions and helpmates. Existing wives have a controlling say in who may become an additional wife.

Varnell takes a poke at polygamy by telling us that "women in third world nations – and southern Utah – who have left polygamous households describe them as rife with favoritism, rivalries, domestic abuse, and the like," which could pass for a fair description of gay relationships as well, with one in every three gays and lesbians experiencing domestic violence. In any case, an exit poll of unhappy people fleeing relationships is hardly a balanced and dispassionate analysis. The sight of a homosexual trying to sell us homosexual wedlock by bad-mouthing polygamy is hypnotically weird.

Chapter Seventeen

Gays Trash the Moral Matrix

The true challenge to America is not simply the issue of gay marriage, but the moral implications of an ever expanding homosexual comfort zone. That comfort zone has been expanding at an accelerating rate ever since that summer evening in 1948 when Harry Hay, a gay Communist Party activist and closeted pedophile, first re-imagined homosexuals as an "oppressed people." Harry wanted all of America to imagine homosexuals as Karl Marx might have imagined homosexuals if Karl Marx had been a homosexual. Harry's bogus paradigm has been the cause of much mischief ever since. This chapter will demonstrate a few of the ways in which the infiltration of gay perspectives is weakening traditional American social institutions, such as our churches, our schools, and the American workplace.

An American Church in Decline

The Episcopal Church is a spare shadow of its former glorious self. Its membership is in steep decline. An emergency panel called the Lambeth Commission struggled with the question of how to keep the 77 million-strong Anglican Communion from bursting apart. Their report was dominated by the challenge of homosexuality which intensified in November 2003 with the ordination of the cheerily homosexual V. Gene Robinson as bishop of New Hampshire. Many traditionalists among the 38 autonomous churches of the Anglican Communion believed this ordination to be a direct attack on 2,000 years of Christian teaching and a flippant disregard of biblical black-letter law.

"We are not in crisis," said the Rev. Martin Reynolds, a spokesman for the liberal Lesbian and Gay Christian Movement. "It is the people who find homosexuality unacceptable who are in crisis." He had a point, sort of. What many traditionalists cannot accept is the paradigm of homosexuality as a new *normal*. Anglican conservatives far outnumber liberals. A 1998 conference of all Anglican bishops flatly declared homosexual behaviors

137

"incompatible with Scripture" and opposed gay ordinations and same-sex blessings by a vote of 526 to 70, with 45 abstentions.

The report by the Anglican Communion's Lambeth Commission advised American Episcopal bishops to stop their priests from blessing same-sex unions. The report declared that the American Episcopal Church should express regret for consecrating an actively homosexual person as a bishop and should not appoint as bishops anyone "living in a same-sex union" until a church consensus emerges. That's not going to happen any time soon.

The emergency Lambeth conference report was commissioned by the Archbishop of Canterbury, Rowan Williams, who was the titular spiritual leader of the 77 million-member Anglican Communion, after a heated gathering of church leaders at Lambeth Palace in London at which many churchmen threatened to sever all ties to the Episcopal Church, as the Anglican Church is called in America, because of the consecration of V. Gene Robinson.

The Lambeth report made no judgments about the morality of homosexuality. Its criticism was aimed at the wayward actions of the American Episcopal Church, which were beyond the horizon of any church consensus on homosexuality and were, therefore, damaging church unity. In the words of the report: "The consecration [of Robinson] has had very prejudicial consequences. In our view, those involved did not pay due regard, in the way they might and, in our view, should have done, to the wider implications of the decisions they were making and the actions they were taking." In other words, consecrating an openly-gay male who had hoodwinked an innocent woman into a bogus marriage, fathered children, and then popped out of his weird psycho-sexual closet to announce his "liberation" as a proud homosexual, was a spectacularly stupid public relations blunder by the gay-loving American Episcopal Church.

The 93-page report said that the people who consecrated Robinson, a gang that included the Episcopal Church's Presiding Bishop Frank Griswold, should have considered "withdraw[ing] themselves from representative functions" of the church until they expressed regret. The report went on to lament the decision of the Canadian province of New Westminster to approve of blessings for homosexual unions. The report made clear that flouting its recommendations could result in expulsion from the Anglican Communion.

In response to the report, the then-presiding bishop of the Episcopal Church, Frank Griswold, penned a terse masterpiece of political mumbo jumbo, saying that his American Episcopalians cared for their communion with other Anglicans and that he regrets "how difficult and painful actions of our church have been to many provinces of our Communion, and the negative repercussions that have been felt by brother and sister Anglicans." In other words, Griswold was only regretful that his actions caused distress to the backward rubes in the African bush and to all those primitive folk who have yet to catch up to his fast-moving avant-garde. Conspicuously absent from Griswold's letter was any acknowledgement of the Lambeth report's recommendation to stop blessing the union of homosexuals.

The Rev. Liz Kaeton of the Church of St. Paul in Chatham, New Jersey, who had voted to support Robinson and the blessing of homosexual unions in her capacity as a member of the Newark diocese's House of Deputies, acknowledged that the American wing of the Anglican church had misjudged the depth of feeling about homosexuality on the rest of the planet. "We had no idea that it was going to cause this kind of pain around the Communion," said the clueless Reverend Kaeton. "I'm certainly willing to say that for causing that kind of pain, I certainly regret that and I'm sorry for it, but I don't regret that he was consecrated."

The Reverend Kaeton's regret is just as shallow as that of Bishop Griswold. To all of these liberals Gene Robinson is the perfect model of a modern major Episcopal leader. They can't imagine why *anyone* might see Robinson as a blundering, self-serving, manipulative, woman-abusing, sexually-confused mischief maker whose life-long dishonesty utterly disqualified him as the spiritual leader of any normal human. He talked pretty; he seemed earnest; he grinned constantly; that was good enough for the progressives.

The Reverend Brian Laffler of St. Anthony of Padua of Hackensack, NJ, said the report "is like putting a Band-Aid on a hemorrhage." His church was the first in New Jersey to request spiritual guidance from another bishop in another diocese. "I don't think it's addressed the larger-reaching question, that there are two entirely diametrically opposed ideologies that are pretty much irreconcilable." That's right, and one of those ideologies is a newfangled and whimsical ideology that is a menace to social cohesion.

The Dawn of the Global South

Christians are a large and varied family. Some people place the spiritual center of their faith in Rome, some in Canterbury, some in Istanbul or Salt Lake City, but one fact is incontrovertible: the population center of global Christianity has shifted to somewhere in the vicinity of Timbuktu. The center of gravity of this faith is moving ever southward. By the year 2100 it should have settled somewhere in northern Nigeria. In the future, the Anglican Communion, and most of all Christian groups, will be energized by the rapidly growing churches of the global South. The demographics are irresistible. Over half of the world's Anglicans are African, and that percentage will swell to 70% by the year 2025, and that's just the African portion of the global South.

Christianity began in the Holy Land, crept westward into Europe and then turned south around the year 1900 thanks to the efforts of European missionaries. By the year 1970 the demographic balance of the Christian world had tipped into Africa and was moving southward. In the decade from 1990 to 2000 the growth rate of Anglicanism in Africa was a robust 2.95 percent, better than Asia's 1.97 percent. By contrast, the European growth rate was a meager 0.13 percent and in North America a sorry *negative* 0.33 percent. The American Episcopal Church is withering. Within a century the 2.8 *billion* Christians south of the equator will number more than three times the 755 million in the global North. These south-of-the-equator Christians are overwhelmingly conservative in their religious perspective, which means that liberal American congregations will become increasingly estranged and isolated from most of the Christian world in the future.

At a General Conference meeting of the United Methodist Church, this declining denomination increased its membership by one million, all of them from the Ivory Coast. Almost every African delegate to this meeting spoke approvingly of continuing that church's ban on homosexual clergy. In Sweden, conservative Lutherans who disdain homosexual wedlock have established a breakaway diocese which is overseen by a Kenyan bishop. There is speculation among Catholics that a future pope could be an African; some are betting on Cardinal Francis Arinze of Nigeria.

American conservatives are saying that the African churches have a firmer grasp of Christian essentials than does the ever-accommodating liberal West. Traditionalists smile at the rich irony of Africa sending missionaries to America.

The Anglican Rev. William Thompson, pastor of All Saints' Church in Long Beach, CA, sought to shelter his congregation under a Ugandan bishop. Three Southern California parishes have ditched the Diocese of Los Angeles, have dropped the word Episcopal from their names and have sought the spiritual guidance of the Ugandan bishop. In the words of the Rev. Thompson: "The American church is going to have to come to grips with the vitality and strength of the global South if it's going to survive as an Anglican entity in any meaningful way."

The Reverend Ian Douglas, professor of world mission and global Christianity at Episcopal Divinity School in Cambridge, Mass., asks, "Do I believe that churches in the global South live with a deep awareness of being part of the gift of a worldwide family of churches? I think they do, and they do it better than we do. That's one reason why we got ourselves into this hot water."

Traditionalists who were chagrined by the consecration of the flagrantly homosexual V. Gene Robinson as bishop of New Hampshire now look to Nigerian Archbishop Peter Akinola and prelates in Malaysia and Argentina for spiritual guidance. Akinola has stated clearly that neither his church nor American traditionalists would accept the Episcopal Church's embrace of the gay social agenda. "We no longer need to look to Canterbury to become Christians," explained Akinola while on an American tour. "If they want to create a new religion, good luck to them, but we don't want a new religion. What we have already is good enough for us."

Peter Akinola is the leader of more than 17 million Anglicans. He is also the chairman of the Council of Anglican Provinces, which embraces more than 37 million members. The global Anglican Communion includes about 77 million members, of which American Episcopalians are a mere 2 million.

"I didn't write the Bible," said the archbishop. "It's part of our Christian heritage. It tells us what to do." To the argument that there was no understanding in biblical times that homosexuality was inborn, and not a mere lifestyle choice, Peter Akinola responded that this approach to Scripture broadcast the offensive message that the Bible "is only for the primitive people."

He further contended that the then-head of the American Episcopal Church, Presiding Bishop Frank Griswold, who had led Robinson's consecration ceremony, could have used his influence to reverse course, but instead made the conscious choice to promote an invasive infiltration of gay countercultural values into the church. "He is a promoter of this whole agenda," Akinola said. "He is accountable to nobody. All that Frank and these people have today is confusion, and they're creating a new religion." One gay group within the Episcopal Church has estimated that as many as one in three Episcopalian clergy are now homosexuals.

This is a *demonstration* of the transformation of a once great church by a determined program of gay colonization which has set that church on a course toward marginalization and declining membership. The Episcopal bishop at the center of the Anglican Communion's global battle over homosexuality, V. Gene Robinson, said the Lambeth report "took my breath away." He would not admit that his consecration ceremony had been staged

142

by a cabal of like-minded radical revisionists, but claimed instead that he would not consider stepping down because, he said, he believed his election to be the work of the Holy Spirit. Robinson declared the language of the report to be "nuanced" so that priests could continue to bless gay couples in private. "So there's some wiggle room there," Robinson said.

Archbishop Peter Akinola did not want to hear any mincing chat about "wiggle room." "Where is the language of rebuke?" asked the archbishop. "It [the report] fails to confront the reality that a small, economically privileged group of people has sought to subvert the Christian faith and impose their new and false doctrine on the wider community of faithful believers." Indeed. And an institution that at one time could be relied upon to solidly support and encourage traditional family life has become an institution that considers traditional family life to be just one of many equally okay New Age lifestyle choices. Thank God for the Africans.

How the Clergy Legitimizes Homosexuality

The power of the clergy to legitimize human pair bonding is solidly established in the popular psyche. It is for this reason that most marriages include a religious ceremony, even though the couple may have already been joined in a civil ceremony. It is also for this reason that homosexuals, including a large and growing gay clergy, are pushing hard to popularize the blessing of homosexual unions.

A glowing article in the *New York Times* tells us that many gays are "sidestepping the debate over legal rights and seeking to consecrate their unions in churches and synagogues," and "they are seeking to have their relationships blessed not by the government, but by God."

The article goes on to explain how ministers and rabbis are eagerly responding to the demand for gay blessings. We are informed that the United Church of Christ is holding workshops for clergy who want to learn how to stage consecration and legitimization ceremonies for homosexuals. The article helpfully adds that a rite for blessing homosexual unions was carefully crafted by the Episcopal Church of New Westminster, British Columbia, and is being widely shared by non-Episcopalian clergy using e-mail. This rite is used as a model for gay-friendly liturgies. The *Times* tells us that "members of the clergy across the country said in interviews that the ceremonies were becoming more common in their churches and synagogues."

Says Rabbi Sharon Gladstone, "I was ordained last year, and the first marriage I officiated at was a marriage of two women. I think that more and more rabbis are officiating, certainly in the Reform and Reconstructionist movements." From the *Times*: "Even some members of the clergy who do not have the permission of their denominations say they are quietly officiating at ceremonies in defiance of their church leaders." It doesn't occur to them that in the very act of consecrating and legitimizing homosexual relationships they are inventing a new religion. More to the point, the *Times* relates that "Although denominations that do permit these rituals formally refer to them as holy unions, same-sex blessings, covenants, or commitment ceremonies, more and more of the couples *and members of the clergy* are simply calling them marriages." [Emphasis added]

These services are often "nearly identical to the marriage rites traditionally used for heterosexual couples." These are marriage *parodies*; nonetheless they work to legitimize the notion of homosexual wedlock in the popular mind. They are parodies as propaganda. The Reverend Fitzgerald says that, "In most cases, we use the same vows and prayers, the same scriptural references. The only thing we change is that we say 'partners' instead of 'husband' and 'wife'."

Those denominations that gladly perform these mock weddings include the ever-elastic Unitarian Universalists, the Disciples of Christ, the United Church of Christ, the Metropolitan Community Churches, and the Reform and Reconstructionist branches of Judaism. Dioceses of the Episcopal Church have been experimenting with gay-blessing rituals. The Presbyterian Church in America allows unlimited blessings of homosexual unions so long as no one actually calls them marriages out loud.

So the clergy are now enthusiastically advancing the gay agenda: they are hell bent to expand the gay comfort zone; they are conforming to the game plan of Marshall Kirk and Hunter Madsen by "muddying the moral waters" and "making gays look good." No thought is given to the fact that gays, collectively, comprise a counterculture whose common values are inimical to a healthy heterosexual society. By legitimizing these unusual relationships the clergy, as exemplars of what is proper, are distorting the moral matrix – that constellation of nurturing social institutions that were created for the protection of traditional marriages and families.

Chapter Eighteen

The Gay Agenda Goes to College

Our schools have always been places of moral instruction, even as contemporary educators deny that they are teaching morals. Every school is a culture unto itself and every culture has its own values. In the interest of self-preservation we should inquire about the values being taught to our society's young people in our schools.

Many colleges have begun recruiting efforts aimed specifically at what one *Newark Star Ledger* article called "the increasingly visible gay and lesbian student market." We are told that "schools from San Jose State to Brown and Harvard" are conducting such targeted recruitment; some prominently feature homosexuals in their brochures. Other colleges, such as American University in Washington, DC, "have carefully cultivated a reputation among high school counselors as being comfortable for gay students," according to the *Star Ledger*.

Representatives from almost 40 New England colleges attended the first-ever college fair for homosexual students, held in Boston. The acknowledged "bible" of college admissions officers, the Journal of College Admissions, featured a cover article about recruiting homosexuals.

Homosexuals have historically chosen colleges based on word of mouth or the visibility of gay and lesbian groups on campus. But with an ever more permissive environment encouraging gays to identify themselves at ever younger ages, colleges have begun getting inquiries about the vitality of gay life on campus. Enter the Gay, Lesbian and Straight Education Network with their college guide for lesbian, gay, bisexual and transgender students. Their first printing of "Finding an LGBT-Friendly Campus" vanished almost as soon as the ink was dry, as students and counselors snatched it up. The Network's public policy director, Mary Kate Cullen, said that gay students who have come from supportive high schools expect a similar atmosphere at college. So these students come to college with a sense of entitlement; they expect the campus culture to accept their signature quirkiness.

The Network encourages gay students to ask how many openly gay students, professors and administrators are on campus and whether there are gay-studies courses or majors offered. Gays are instructed to ask whether there are support services for homosexuals and whether the campus includes active clubs and student organizations for gays and lesbians, which can be used to exert influence on the administration.

No college in America is more accepting of all things homosexual than Drew University in Madison, New Jersey. Drew placed first in the Princeton Review's national student survey, narrowly edging out Boston U, Wesleyan, Wellesley and Vassar as havens for homosexuals. Every year Drew celebrates National Coming Out Day and bombards its students with seminars titled "Everything You Wanted to Know About Being Gay But Were Afraid to Ask," which unfold in the freshman dorms. Speaking of the Princeton Review's assessment of his school, Drew spokesman Tom Harris demurely said, "We almost never use those rankings for marketing." Gee, why not, Tom?

According to an article in the *Boston Globe* (5/21/02), college admissions officers believe that students who have gone through the coming-out process in high school have more self-confidence, more leadership abilities, more cultural awareness and other superior qualities than those plain old run-of-the-mill heterosexual kids. The *Globe* quoted Judith Brown, director of Lesbian Gay Bisexual Transgender Center at Tufts University: "Schools are inviting these students because they question norms...They make people question their own assumptions, and that's key to learning and growing as people."

And yet..., norms and shared assumptions are central to the stability of a shared culture which, in turn, is vital to the preservation of a nurturing civilization. Homosexuals are a splinter-group sexuality or, more correctly, a collection of splinter-group sexualities. Their challenges to society's norms are the yapping of a few peevish misfits; their desire to restructure our society could easily be ignored if it weren't for the liberals, who were born to pander. For example . . .

The Dawn of the Coed Dorm Room

First came the coeducational college, then came coed dormitories, followed by the mixed-gender bathroom. Now, in a gush of gay friendliness, comes the mixed-gender dorm room. The *New York Times* (5/11/02) informs us that this departure from tradition "is less about sex than sexual politics – and the increasingly powerful presence of gay and lesbian groups on campus," groups nurtured by the colleges themselves.

It seems the big push to abolish prohibitions against mixed-gender dorm rooms came from homosexuals who declared such traditional decorum to be "heterosexist." That was all the liberal administrators at places such as Swarthmore and Haverford College needed to hear; it was like an incantation they could not resist. And the problem? *Gay* students were uncomfortable sharing living space with a roommate of the same sex.

The campaign at Haverford was begun by a 2000 graduate named Josh Andrix who explained: "Straight men who live together often have a locker-room mentality, with a lot of discussion about dating girls, having sex with girls, saying which girls are attractive. Introducing a homosexual into that environment is uncomfortable. When I looked for housing, all the people it made sense for me to live with were women." So, a male who isn't really a man feels uncomfortable in the culture of men. He disparages their banter as reflective of a "locker-room mentality." Are women displaying a locker-room mentality when *they* chat about dating and cute guys? Josh doesn't say.

"In three to five years coed housing will be an option on most campuses," says Myrt Westphal, Swarthmore's director of residential life. She adds, "Students like the option." No surprise there.

So, to accommodate some uncomfortable homosexuals, schools will demolish the last barrier to on-campus mixed-gender cohabitation. The change is made to please a few oddballs and the moral consequences for young heterosexuals, who comprise the overwhelming majority of students, is momentous. The colonization of campuses by politically savvy gays has warped the moral matrix in which heterosexual students on those campuses must live.

On some campuses homosexuals have preferred to isolate themselves in housing all their own. The University of Hartford offers separate housing for students involved in Spectrum, its group for lesbian, bisexual, gay and transgender students. At the University of Massachusetts the same sorts live on the "Two in Twenty" floor. Wesleyan University offers Open House, which the school calls a residence for the "queer, questioning, and those interested in queer culture." Got that? *Queer culture*, which is something distinctly alien to the culture of almost everyone else.

Young people, and especially young women, who are away from home for the first time, were better served by traditional campus living arrangements, in a time when college administrations behaved like adults who understood that the decorum of heterosexual norms was an exercise in hard-won wisdom.

Schools in the Twilight Zone

The razor's edge of weird campus activism is brought to us by the transgender students who have convinced colleges to accommodate them with private bathrooms and showers, specialized housing and specialized sports teams on which players need not identify themselves as either male or female. Four East Coast colleges, including Wesleyan, Smith and Sarah Lawrence, have already rolled over for the trannies.

Transgender folk are uncomfortable with the gender of their birth. Some transgender students may also be simulacra – surgically-altered replicas of the gender they imagine themselves to be, in

150

which case they may also be called transsexuals. Some students are only part way through this remodeling process.

The transgendered have abandoned themselves to a thought disorder: they imagine themselves to be some gender other than the one their naked selves says that they are. They have a problem with gender identity, which is distinct from sexual orientation. Sexual orientation is all about which gender a person is attracted to; gender identity is all about which gender a person imagines himself/herself to be. A goodly number of transgender students prefer to remain parked somewhere between identifiable genders and prefer to call themselves "gender queer."

At Wesleyan, students who were born female but who have affected male dress and mannerisms may have a genuine male roommate. The school's former women's rugby team dropped the word "women's" from its name so that several born-female transgender folk would feel more comfortable. The campus health clinic no longer requires that students check off an M or an F box on the clinic health form.

At Brown University, freshmen are allowed to elect a gender-neutral option on the housing questionnaire. They can sequester themselves in dorms with lockable bathrooms that accommodate only one person. This is the school's solution to girls who think that they are guys but who aren't usually accepted as such in the big bathroom with the urinals.

The *New York Times* regales us with tales of several gender-bending females and the colleges that enable their fixations, in an article titled "On College Campuses, Rethinking Biology 101." Here we meet "Zachary," a strapping lass who can't pass for male despite her best efforts. She says she suffered harassment at her Pittsburgh high school. "I ended up threatening to sue the school for not protecting me," she whines. It never enters her close-cropped head that her deliberately provocative deportment had predictably prompted commentary from her adolescent peers. It never occurs to her that her insistence that she too is a man is an insult to every genuine man to whom she says it. A man is a vessel of masculine virtue; a pushy female transgender freak acting out a grotesque parody of genuine manhood is an empty suit.

Next we are introduced to Paige, whose efforts to look masculine have only made her look middle-aged. She rooms with a male who is "extremely respectful." When referring to Paige he uses only pronouns approved by the transgender community: "ze" instead of "he" or "she," and "hir" instead of "him" or "her."

The one thing all of these wishful dreamers have in common is their desire to have the whole world be exquisitely attuned to their emotional needs. Only in the synthetic utopian theme parks called American colleges would so many people work so hard to cater to such weird desires. Wesleyan's medical director of student health services, Dr. Davis Smith, said that "On this campus transgender students are real opinion leaders." No doubt.

At Smith, a women's college, students chose to eliminate all female pronouns from the student constitution at the request of transgender students. The words "she" and "her" were tossed out in favor of "the student." The students did this as a gesture of good will, to be *nice*. But the true import of the gesture was not lost on sophomore Esi Cleland who exclaimed, "It contradicts the whole point of having a women's college. I am opposed to it, because there's something to be said for a women's college, and a lot of us come here because we choose to be in an environment where women are the primary focus."

Exactly! A women's college should nurture *feminine* virtue, *women's* values and women's culture. Why on Earth would they mutilate their constitution to accommodate a handful of females who imagine themselves to be **men**? It's a creepy gesture, a sort of symbolic female circumcision. Once again a perfectly healthy dimension of the moral matrix has been warped to accommodate the esoteric needs of a not-so-healthy handful of unhappy people.

152

Teaching Gayness at Your Expense

Taxpayer-funded colleges will even teach wondering freshmen how to be more fully homosexual. For example, at the University of Michigan, a public university, Professor Davis Halperin enthusiastically teaches a course called "How to be Gay: Male Homosexuality and Initiation." The syllabus explains that "Just because you happen to be a gay man doesn't mean you don't have to learn how to become one. Gay men do some of that learning on their own, but, often, we learn how to be gay from others."

Should taxpayers be funding gay initiations? Professor Halperin says of his course offering: "It does not teach students to be homosexual. Rather, it examines critically the odd notion that there are right and wrong ways to be gay, that homosexuality is not just a sexual practice or desire, but a set of specific tastes in music, movies, and other cultural forms." In other words, it's a crash course in the gay subculture. The syllabus goes so far as to use the word "indoctrination." Need I add that this subculture has always fancied itself to be adversarial and subversive to the values of normal nurturing heterosexual culture?

Chapter Nineteen

The Arrogance of the Self-Anointed

If gays don't arrive at college already endowed with an exquisitely sensitive sense of victimhood, then the college administration, the activist faculty and the already entrenched student political groups will conspire to imbue the gay freshman with just such a touchy disposition. On campus, gays *aspire* to victim status. The much-coveted goal of victim status is not, heaven forbid, to suffer any real oppression, but rather to seize the opportunity to mine that rich vein of solid-gold self-righteousness that is so treasured by would-be secular saints and melodramatic political martyrs.

In their scramble to secure the lowest rung on the ladder, political gays on campus must compete with political blacks, Hispanics, feminists, et al. The bright badge of victimhood shields gays from criticism; it puts their critics on the defensive; it allows them to intimidate the vast hetero majority. The self-anointed victim thus becomes a self-appointed defender of gay pride, an object of sympathy immune to sanction and someone free to bludgeon all political opponents with a diagnosis of "homophobia."

Most American universities have already watered down or dumped the greatest works of Western thought to create a favored place for new course offerings in racial and gender studies, including a rapidly expanding literature in gay studies and "queer theory." Because gays now strike a pose of studied touchiness, the university bosses discourage the faculty from offering any factual material that might provoke a protest. Professors who are too candid have found themselves the targets of organized vilification and administrative sanction. These taboos do not apply to overtly ideological queer theorists who are immune to criticism.

The left-wing academy also expresses its political opinions through its professional associations. For example, back in 1987 the Modern Language Association, an association of university humanities scholars, passed this resolution: "Be it therefore resolved that the MLA will refrain from locating future

155

conventions not already scheduled in any state that has criminalized acts of sodomy through legislation. . ." Was this altruism, or a fear of arrest?

Universities now promote "pluralism" and "diversity" by permitting and funding separate institutions and "theme houses" for minorities, including homosexuals. Ironically, this isolationism shields these minorities from genuine pluralism. The imposition of sanctions for any utterance that tweaks the sensitivity of anyone who is not white or heterosexual regarding matters of race, gender and sexual orientation does not encourage inter-group socializing. As members of a presumed victim class, blacks, feminists and homosexuals are now exempt from these suffocating speech codes, which include such offenses as "disparaging facial expressions" and "inappropriate laughter."

For example, graduate student Jerome Pinn arrived at his University of Michigan dorm room to discover that his new roommate had festooned the walls with photographs of nude men. His assigned roommate told Mr. Pinn point blank that he was a lusty homosexual and that he intended to use their dorm room for sundry homosexual romps. Not surprisingly, Mr. Pinn approached the university housing office with a polite request for a different room assignment. Mr. Pinn recalls that "They were outraged by this. They asked me what was wrong with me – what *my* problem was. I said that I had a religious and moral objection to homosexual conduct. They were surprised; they couldn't believe it. Finally they agreed to assign me to another room, but they warned me that if I told anyone of the reason, I would face university charges of discrimination on the bases of sexual orientation."

Students in some schools have endured re-education sessions that included forced apologies, the denigration of their religious beliefs and the compulsory viewing of gay pornographic films in misguided attempts to make them more "sensitive" to the emotional needs of homosexuals.

In 1988, the law school faculty of the State University of New York at Buffalo adopted a resolution that included warnings to students to avoid "remarks directed at another person's...sexual preference." Violators, the law faculty warned, could not expect protection under the First Amendment because "our intellectual community shares values that go beyond a mere standardized commitment to open and unrestrained debate." The law faculty warned that it would take "strong and immediate steps" to punish anyone who uttered an offensive word and that as defenders of homosexuals they would "not be limited solely to the use of ordinary university procedures," but might go so far as to send letters to "any bar to which such a student applies" that would include "our conclusion that the student should not be admitted to practice law." In other words, if you sniff at a homosexual the law faculty just might destroy your future.

Over time, the use of such policies has increased the proportion of gay-friendly judges who now sit in judgment of such issues as gay marriage, gay adoption rights, and gay hiring quotas. The current strategy of gay litigators, such as the Lambda Legal Defense Fund, is to "judge shop" from state to state in the hope of finding those judges who will impose the gay agenda on America by judicial fiat. The more such judges there are, the better are the chances for a total gay triumph. It was the self-identified homosexual judge Vaughn Walker who struck down California's the voter-approved constitutional amendment defining marriage in the ancient manner, as the union of one man and one woman.

The University of Connecticut has a policy on harassment that imposes penalties, including expulsion, for offenses such as "the use of derogatory names," "inconsiderate jokes," "misdirected laughter," and "conspicuous exclusion from conversation." This same university places no restraints on the sexual conduct of its students, including homosexuals. The school handbook says that "the university shall not regard itself as the arbiter or enforcer of the morals of the students."

Yale University sports at least five gay and lesbian groups, including one exclusively for Chicano lesbians. Yale's gays are loud and proud; their annual gay/lesbian ball may attract over a thousand revelers. When the *Wall Street Journal* took note of the fact that Yale had acquired a gay reputation, Yale's then-president Benno Schmidt, shot off a letter to fund raisers denying that Yale was a "gay school" and assuring alumni that if there were any truth to the allegation that "I would be concerned too."

That's all Yale's powerful gay lobby needed to hear; gay activists swamped Mr. Schmidt with demands to know what was wrong with Yale being a very gay school. The best the apologetic Mr. Schmidt could muster was some unconvincing gibberish about the need to have a proportional number of heterosexuals at Yale to maintain the cherished goal of "diversity."

The explosive expansion of the gay comfort zone on American campuses has been a top-down affair. It is today's gay and liberal administrators who have been most influential in promoting the gay colonization of campus communities, not activist students who comprise this revolution's vocal but comparatively powerless youth corps. It is sympathy from above that has allowed the thorough-going infiltration of gay ideology into institutions that are now bent on undermining traditional American folkways. In many cases, profound changes have been made without any student demands. These changes are important to all of us because our universities are not mere mirrors of our society, they are incubators of social fashions and culture-transforming paradigms – they are leading indicators of what our larger society will become.

Few environments surpass the intimacy of campus life. After four years of accommodation to gender-bending classmates, queer theorists, and a multicultural habitat that endorses the equality of *all* modes of conduct, many students are unable to recognize just how weird their campus community truly is. These captive students have been the subjects of a radical social experiment to which they did not consent. The rules were not theirs to make.

After graduation, *every* former student will have an opinion about homosexual relationships and the worthiness of gay marriage and gay adoption and gay parenting, even as national surveys demonstrate that a majority of these same graduates cannot identify Shakespeare and Milton with their major works and are clueless about the import of the Magna Carta and Reconstruction. Fully one in four college seniors has no idea when Columbus set foot in the New World; they confuse the words of the United States Constitution with those of Karl Marx. Thirty-seven percent of American college students are not required to take a single history course. And yet, **all** of them have been exposed to *years* of gay-agenda indoctrination intended to shape their future voting behavior and to weaken their attachment to traditional, time-tested, modes of human conduct. Gender studies and queer theory are part of *every* student's curriculum, whether they desire it or not.

If there is a comical dimension to the multi-culti crowd's love of all things non-Western it is their awkwardness in dealing with Third-World attitudes toward homosexuality. Every culture in the Third World imagines homosexuality to be either a sin or a sickness. Given what the Third World has to offer homosexuals, Western-style tolerance doesn't seem to be such a bad deal.

Nonetheless, strident gays on campus offer little tolerance to those who do not embrace *their* assumptions. At the University of Michigan a student who poked fun at homosexual acts was condemned by the administration to write a public apology titled "Learned My Lesson" for publication in the *Michigan Daily* and to attend Gay Rap sessions. Another student at the same school made the big mistake of suggesting that homosexuality could be "cured." He was charged with gender-based harassment and his comments were subjected to "review by the appropriate social work professionals to evaluate his suitability to be a professional social worker." Once again, those who don't share the enforced orthodoxy of the gay-friendly Left are threatened with the ruination of their lives.

The Suffocating Gay Orthodoxy

Gays on campus are a headache because they want to wield political power while insulating themselves from criticism and open debate. This problem is made worst by administrators who arm these gay political alliances with punitive speech codes. Ordinary heterosexuals on campus now live in the shadow of a de facto Gay Inquisition, even as valid philosophical and moral questions are declared forever off limits for discussion. The university tradition of open inquiry has been tossed away, along with the great works of Western thought. Coercion is not persuasion; it is not a reasoned argument, but it gets the gays what they want.

Suppressing debate on any aspect of the gay agenda de-legitimizes the university. Academic freedom and academic taboos are mutually antagonistic. Either allow a debate about the gay agenda or omit the gay agenda from the school curriculum. Criminalizing argumentation is the hallmark of academic hacks.

The new "diversity" is just a diversity of radical opinions; it is a narrow-spectrum orthodoxy espoused by vocal conformists. If, for example, you believe that a homosexual orientation has no moral implications, then you are "for diversity." If you hold any other opinion, then you are "against diversity," and are deserving of sanctions. The heretic must be heckled and ostracized.

The constant browbeating and dishonest double standards try the patience of even the most sympathetic student. When impatience finally turns to anger, the guardians of "minority rights" are quick to charge that all resentments are the result of lurking homophobia; they see every contradiction of gay orthodoxy as a sure sign that they have been lax in their defense of minorities; after that they vow to tighten the screws even more.

By junior or senior year the "heightened consciousness" of self-righteous homosexuals may have congealed into a sticky dogmatism. The sensitive gay freshman has become a gay-rights monitor conducting political surveillance in all of his classroom settings. Professors may praise these spies as exemplars of just the sort of "diversity" that gays contribute to the classroom. The gay monitors of gay orthodoxy are flattered to have their "superior consciousness" acknowledged.

Worse yet, the forced celebration of splinter-group sexualities, gender confusion, and oddball obsessions is an arrogant imposition on almost every tuition-paying customer. Almost everyone in America has a heterosexual destiny to fulfill; life's early years should be spent in preparation to fulfill that destiny. The burden is on the folks with abnormal proclivities to find a niche for themselves somewhere in the grand scheme of our great civilization. The greater society is not obligated to transform itself in any way that will diminish its first purpose: to maintain the health of its moral matrix, which is to say, all of its interdependent, life-sustaining social institutions: its religions, its schools, its marriages and a host of affiliated associations, such as charities, fraternal organizations and children's groups.

The greater society is no more obligated
to *celebrate* homosexuality than it is to celebrate any of a thousand other paraphilias. Shall we all celebrate shoe fetishists or panty sniffers? No? Then why should we celebrate homosexual anal erotics? All that distinguishes gays from other paraphiliacs is their superior public relations efforts. The "gay community" is really no more than an ad hoc conglomeration of small-time sexualities that coheres for a single reason: political expediency. If these strange people with their strange predilections did not need one another politically, they would not be on speaking terms. All of the sexual-minority factions (gay, lesbian, transvestite, pederast, fetish-obsessed and totally delusional) are freakishly small; all of them are the result of some developmental mishap. Their modes of behavior are unfit models for heterosexuals; they have nothing to teach normal heterosexuals about how to be better heterosexuals, which is our one and only healthy destiny.

It's time to tell the gay bullies that they are tiresome, that gay is not avant-garde, that the rest of us have more important things to do than listen to their incessant bitching.

Chapter Twenty

Gays in the Workplace

No sooner has the American student graduated from college than he comes under the watchful eye of the gay-friendly corporate Thought Police. Historically, employers have not encouraged homosexuals in their employ to be open and expressive in their homosexuality. In fact, muting *everyone's* sexual expressiveness has been the traditional corporate tack. In short, bland was beautiful. Not any more. Rolf Szabo found that out the hard way.

Mr. Szabo had been a loyal employee of the Eastman Kodak Corporation for twenty-three years when, out of the blue, his boss sent him an e-mail promoting something called "Coming Out Day." This memo included instructions for assisting closeted homosexuals to "come out" in the workplace. Mr. Szabo was urged to acknowledge the "courage" of homosexuals in being more expressively gay. Mr. Szabo was instructed to "be sensitive to the [gay] employee's language in defining their personal orientation" and "share your personal willingness to understand." The message also instructed Mr. Szabo to monitor other employees for any anti-gay comments or humor. The memo included a warning to "keep in mind that such behaviors violate Kodak Values as well as Kodak's Equal Opportunity Employment Policy, which all supervisors are responsible for maintaining in their areas . . . Reported violations of this policy are to be thoroughly investigated. If verified, disciplinary action is to be taken."

Mr. Szabo did not warm to the Big-Brother tone of the memo. Neither did he care to play midwife and nanny to nominal adults who were struggling with abnormal sexuality issues. He replied to his boss' memo with one of his own requesting that his boss never again send him such a memo because he considered it offensive. With a click of the wrong button he also sent his memo to everyone who had gotten his boss' original memo.

163

Mr. Szabo's boss responded by flashing an e-mail to everyone on his mailing list. He apologized for Mr. Szabo's e-mail. In the interest of tolerance he demanded that everyone adopt the corporation's social values. Intoned the boss: "While I understand that we are all free to have our own personal beliefs, when we come to the Kodak workplace, our behaviors must align with the Kodak Values. I apologize for the e-mail sent to all of you from Rolf Szabo this morning. Rolf's comments are hurtful to our employees, friends, and family members who are gay, lesbian, bisexual, or transgendered. This behavior is not aligned with the Kodak Values and, therefore, is not acceptable."

Subsequently, the company insisted that Mr. Szabo apologize in writing for calling his boss' e-mail "offensive" and promising to never again express his distaste for the company's efforts to expand the gay comfort zone at Kodak. He was told that if he did not comply he would lose his job. Mr. Szabo, a devout Catholic, refused to recant his honest opinion. Kodak fired him.

To this day, Kodak brags about its tolerance and inclusion and diversity, but a diversity of radical opinions is not true diversity and demonizing principled employees is overt intolerance. Drafting employees to assist strangers in their personal struggles with their sexual quirks is just plain bad manners. Will Kodak continue to enlarge its list of emotionally needy folks to include those with ever stranger proclivities? What about the emotional needs of rubber fetishists? What about transvestites who want to strut their stuff in the workplace? What's the rationale for excluding them? Should a corporation transform itself into a clinic for the benefit of *anyone* with a quirk and then draft its normal employees as amateur therapists for the benefit of the quirky folk?

Would Kodak *ever* consider having a Coming Out Day for Christians or Orthodox Jews? Take a wild guess. Kodak Values is just a front for the radical social agenda of the gay theorists Marshall Kirk and Hunter Madsen. Kodak Values fulfills the objectives of the Kirk & Madsen game plan because it strives to 1. "Talk about gays," 2. "Portray gays as victims," 3. "Give protectors a just cause," 4. "Make gays look good," and 5. "Make the victimizers look bad." In its zeal to promote the black-letter text of the gay agenda, Kodak goes so far as to terminate employees who won't play along.

The truth is that gays get preferential treatment because their clout intimidates employers who fear bad publicity and costly litigation. If Christians sued to preserve their dignity and religious freedom, then employers would fear **them**.

Rolf Szabo brought a lawsuit against Eastman Kodak for violating his religious freedom. Kodak has certainly demonstrated its intolerance of true diversity, as opposed to a mere diversity of radical opinions. Employees at AT&T and Verizon are also suing their employers for violating their religious beliefs with coerced pledges to respect and value homosexual behaviors.

Imposing Gay Values from Above

As in the case of universities, the Kodak Corporation is imposing a radical social agenda on its employees from above. Sixty percent of homosexual adults hold professional positions; they are disproportionately represented among the clergy, the professoriate, and the lawyering class. Gays may also have infiltrated the highest ranks of Eastman Kodak, Verizon and AT&T.

The standard boilerplate defense for why Kodak would encourage gays to be more expressive in the workplace, while discouraging Christians and Jews from doing the same, is that Christian and Jewish expressiveness is all wrapped up in *values*, whereas gayness is stupidly imagined to be just some benign and value-neutral orientation akin to a preference for chocolate rather than vanilla. This is dangerous hokum.

Kodak Values is an effort to mainstream gay countercultural values in the workplace; it is a program to legitimize homosexuality. Years down the road some of Kodak's *openly* homosexual employees will be sitting in the Kodak boardroom making decisions about future "values" programs that will profoundly affect the workplace environment of every normal heterosexual employee. The values that Kodak enforces and projects will also affect *other* workplace environments because large corporations like Kodak are *models* for other businesses. Kodak is setting *an example* with its in-house social engineering. Kodak is also telling its employees to check their most cherished beliefs at the door. Will Kodak next use its enormous economic clout to dictate to its smaller suppliers that they too must have gay-friendly workplaces if they want to do business with Kodak?

If you think this last idea is farfetched, then think again. Kodak already has in place its aggressive *Supplier Diversity Program* which has shut out most small businesses owned by anyone of the white race. Established white-race suppliers have seen their volume of business with Kodak severely reduced just because of their race. The remaining white suppliers are compelled to certify to Kodak that they too are imposing an aggressive, race-based program of their own on their second and third tier subcontractors. The white businessmen must certify in writing that they directly employ a number of *persons of color*, or POCs in Kodak-speak. A consequence of this racist program of anti-white preferences is that white-owned businesses were excluded from $200 million of Kodak business. A Kodak annual report gave assurances that "Kodak continues to take aggressive steps to identify and partner with diverse suppliers." So don't imagine for a second that Kodak would not preferentially pour millions of dollars into enterprises controlled by homosexuals, if only they could identify them. That would be millions of dollars that were diverted from the support of traditional workers with traditional families and traditional values.

Clearly, Kodak has been colonized by partisans of the gay agenda. This company is encouraging the expression of gay values in its workplace; it is insisting that its employees monitor each other for any sign of non-compliance with its gay-friendly social program; it is penalizing and firing anyone who resists their radical social engineering.

Mr. Szabo was not fired because he violated any law; he was terminated for not preferring Kodak's gay agenda above his deeply-held Catholic faith. Indeed, Title VII of the Civil Rights Act of 1964 specifically prohibits discrimination based on race, color, sex, religion, or national origin. The word "sex" in Title VII means male or female and makes no legal reference to homosexuality. If an employee wearing a turban must be accommodated, then why was Mr. Szabo compelled to recant his religious beliefs, in writing, or face termination? Mr. Szabo explained: "I would not submit and cave in to their trying to browbeat me into a confession."

Kodak is not alone in its concern over the troubling diversity of thought exhibited by its employees. The corporation-as-behavior-modification-and-re-education camp is alive and thriving. In 2002 Kodak was one of 13 companies that got a perfect 100 percent score in the Human Rights Campaign's first Corporate Equality Index. The HRC is a well-funded gay political organization; its index rates large corporations on their policies toward gays. The HRC gave top marks to Aetna, American Airlines, Apple Computers, Avaya, Intel, J.P.Morgan Chase & Co., Replacements, Inc., Worldspan and Xerox.

Up in Rochester, NY, where Kodak has its headquarters, talk-show host Bob Lonsberry gave Kodak's firing of Rolf Szabo a good airing. Mr. Lonsberry observed, "In the name of tolerance they foment a spirit of intolerance. Their ongoing incessant theme is diversity of the most progressive sort, but those in the workplace feel it's rubbed in their faces." A listener responded on Lonsberry's message board: "I work in the same division as Rolf. Kodak is constantly trying to cram this diversity crap down our throats. We are told by management that all beliefs are welcome. Well, as Rolf found out, if your opinions and fundamental beliefs go against the Kodak party line, you will be gone."

The creepiest thought in all of this is the possibility that the persons who are imposing these re-education programs on normal heterosexuals may be homosexuals. As we have already seen, a spouse and children are not proof that a person is not gay. Millions of homosexuals are masquerading as married straights; many of them now occupy commanding positions in giant corporations. Our schools and corporations have been colonized by people with alien sensibilities; the quality of our lives is being diminished by hidden homosexuals with a deep personal stake in transforming every corner of American life into a gay comfort zone.

The Gay Colonization of Motorola

Motorola got its modest start manufacturing radios for automobiles. It has since grown into a sprawling telecommunications business with worldwide sales of $30 billion. Their name is now affixed to wireless telephones, messaging systems, two-way radios and Internet-access products. Motorola is also engineering another top-down revolution in homosexual power politics; it is yet another rapidly expanding gay comfort zone. This is making a lot of traditional heterosexuals at Motorola *very* uncomfortable.

The management-driven gay-counterculture activism at Motorola includes "homophobia" workshops, homosexual sex education courses, and e-mail recruitment for gay-pride parades. Gay-friendly forces within Motorola have free use of the corporation's e-mail system, its bulletin boards, its televisions, and its meeting rooms and offices for gay seminars and gay film festivals. Of special concern to Motorola employees are the "Homophobia in the Workplace" workshops, one of which a Motorola website deemed "mandatory."

Motorola also supports a website called MotoPride for gay, lesbian, bisexual and transgender people. This site touts the "unconditional" support of Motorola's management team for the homosexual community. The site sketches Motorola's historical commitment to expanding America's gay comfort zone: "1993, Motorola launches the Gay, Bisexual, and Lesbian employee network GABLE-NET to foster discussion of GLBT issues in the workplace; 1994, Mandatory Homophobia in the Workplace workshops are conducted in Plantation, Florida; 1996, Motorola adds sexual orientation to its U.S. non-discrimination policy; 1998,

168

Motorola holds "Homophobia in the Workplace" workshops in Austin, Texas; 1999, Motorola celebrates its first Gay and Lesbian Awareness Day in Austin, Texas and Phoenix, Arizona; 2000 Motorola adds same-gender domestic partner health and dental benefits for U.S. employees; 2002, Motorola partners with Gay.com, PlanetOut.com and the Advocate to celebrate Gay Pride Month with the MotoPRIDE Campaign, supporting pride festivals and events across the nation," and so forth.

A Motorola engineer, who wished to remain anonymous for reasons that will be obvious, gave an interview to WorldNet Daily wherein he described the mood of "quiet anger" among those heterosexual employees who approve of traditional family values. In his words: "The drums of diversity are a great way to get positively recognized by corporate leadership, even though you do little or nothing to contribute to a profitable bottom line of the company. [Co-workers and I] have observed that many less technically competent people get promoted to management by their own 'beating the drums of diversity'" He went on to explain that "the homosexual activists are by far the most feared by management. And, it appears, [they] have free rein of internal media, corporate resources, and event scheduling." He says the straights at Motorola continue to live in "quiet anger" because management has clearly given the gay agenda top priority. Some employees are more equal than others.

Sandia Abuses Christians

At least 300 of America's 500 most powerful companies have gay-friendly employment policies. These policies often exceed a proper insistence on tolerance and civility and become a promotion of homosexual behaviors so aggressive as to discriminate against traditional men and women.

Not to be outdone by corporations, the Sandia National Laboratories in New Mexico discriminates against religious believers daily, while lavishing preferential treatment on homosexuals. Sandia management explicitly forbids people of faith from placing any references to religion or religious events on its

169

bulletin boards. The faithful are prohibited from using computer screen savers with religious content. The bosses demand the removal of all posters, books and pictures with religious content. Sandia management even forbade its engineers from naming a reconnaissance robot Caleb, after the biblical spy. To add an extra sting to their list of anti-traditionalist prohibitions, the normal employees were requested to remove all photos of their spouses and children because **homosexuals** feel uncomfortable displaying photos of *their* intimate relationships.

By contrast, the Sandia administrators can't do enough to encourage the homosexuals at Sandia to be as expressive as possible. Gay values and gay perspectives are promoted at every opportunity. Sandia officially recognizes the Gay/Lesbian/Bisexual Network Group to which it enthusiastically gave "funding, administrative assistance, and use of the company facilities and communications channels." In other words, the homosexuals were given free rein at Sandia.

In April 2000, Sandia shut down its top-secret facilities for two days in order to corral its employees into "diversity training" sessions. Sandia management subjects its employees to annual "Coming Out Day" celebrations where they are pressured to accept and respect homoerotic behaviors.

Given its commitment to expanding the gay comfort zone at Sandia National Laboratories, it is not surprising that the Sandia management denied recognition to a Christian group. Management merely sniffed at the Christians and told them that they had "not established the existence of workplace barriers based on religion." The Christians, who had been prohibited from any expressiveness and who had even been told to conceal their family photos, begged to differ. Referring to these examples of discrimination, the Christians observed that "many Christian workers are not comfortable with expressing who they are openly for fear of ridicule or reprimand from management or fellow employees."

Sandia management told the Christians to pound sand, so the Christians hired a lawyer and filed a lawsuit. Their attorney,

Stephen Crampton, of the American Family Association, called Sandia's policies toward religious traditionalists "discriminatory against religion on its face. It is an insult not only to believers in God, but to believers in freedom everywhere."

You have been presented with numerous examples of how free expression, traditional sentiments and heterosexual culture are diminished wherever gays control the levers of power. Programs that begin as efforts to gain sympathy for gays by persuasion and familiarization soon degenerate into heavy-handed attempts to reform traditionalists, to make them reconsider their religious beliefs, their ideas about parenting and even their notions about basic hygiene. If "heavy-handed" doesn't do the job, then iron-fisted prohibitions are brought to bear on traditionalists, such as speech codes, mandatory "sensitivity" training, and threats of expulsion, termination, or the ruination of their careers by defamation. Wherever gays or the ideologically-inclined friends of gays achieve dominion over us, the moral matrix that was created to support traditional students, wage earners, and families is distorted to serve the purposes of the homosexual counterculture.

By threatening those traditionalists who are reluctant to re-examine their commitment to the precepts of their religions, their folkways, and even Mom's toilet-training instruction, gays have done nothing but provoke quiet anger and inspire lots of underdog humor aimed at gays. The ever expanding gay comfort zone is making the traditionalist majority feel marginalized and uncomfortable.

When demands are imposed upon ordinary people to tolerate things that are harmful to the health of the very institutions that sustain traditional family life, then intolerance becomes a virtue. Churches, schools, workplaces and private associations that ooze gay values and gay perspectives and a gay sensibility are as useless as a gay bathhouse to those of us who are struggling to maintain traditional lives and traditional families.

We have glimpsed the future that the gay utopians are preparing for us – a world of speech codes, spying co-workers, school expulsions, employment terminations, hiring quotas, preferential

171

treatment, the emergence of a flagrantly gay clergy, the demonization of religious traditionalists, the legitimization of homosexual wedlock, an increase of homoerotic imagery in our popular entertainment, the trivialization of our traditional values, increased gay role modeling in our children's school books and in the classroom, and many other unpleasant surprises. It's a world unrecognizable to our forebears; it's a world in moral disarray, a place of confusion.

Chapter Twenty One

What Is to be Done?

The explosive expansion of the homosexual comfort zone is the consequence of a highly sophisticated and lavishly financed propaganda campaign, all of it clearly articulated in the black-letter texts of the seminal queer theorists Marshall Kirk and Hunter Madsen. This clever gay duo of Harvard-trained persuaders used their insights into human weakness to craft a campaign of seduction to win the support of gullible heterosexuals – those good-hearted people whom the activists on the political Far Left call "the useful idiots."

This propaganda campaign, first outlined by Kirk and Madsen in *The Gay Agenda* in 1985 and later expanded into *The Overhauling of Straight America* in 1987, is a cynical game plan for defrauding and manipulating **normal** Americans. The once obvious-to-everyone essence of the homosexual soul was suddenly hidden behind a curtain of disarming images of homosexuals as folks who are "just as normal" as the ninety-nine percent of humanity who had successfully achieved normal heterosexuality.

Defending the Normal

The best defense against a lie is the truth; sunshine is the best disinfectant. The written script of the gay agenda is a catalog of self-admitted deceptions. Kirk and Madsen boldly coached all homosexuals to **lie** about what gays *really* think, feel and do. The true nature of homosexual behavior is something gays are instructed to **keep hidden** from normal people; the true nature of the homosexual psyche must remain a mystery.

To counter this campaign of falsehoods we defenders of traditional cultural values must create a *meta-narrative* – a truthful narrative *about* the fraudulent gay narrative. The gay manifesto must be "de-constructed" sentence by sentence. Every cynical trick

173

in their unscrupulous bag of tricks must be parsed and explained for the benefit of those uncritical people who were seduced into supporting the gay agenda for shallow emotional reasons.

Workshops must be established to familiarize the average citizen with the subversive scripts of the gay agenda, line by line. Every American must be informed of the long-term consequences of demoting traditional marriage to a co-equal status with newfangled social institutions invented by gays to idealize the unusual emotional chemistries of male and female homosexuals. Whatever else they may be, homosexual unions are not marriages. The reckless Scandinavian campaign to legalize homosexual wedlock ruined the institution of marriage as Norwegians, Swedes and Danes had known it.

Every American should be made aware that gay activists have been subjecting all of us to a program of "desensitization" as scripted by Kirk and Madsen. In their own words: "At least in the beginning, we are seeking public *desensitization* and nothing more." In short, the gay agenda seeks to strip normal humans of their protective suspicions of abnormal sexual behaviors.

"The way to benumb raw sensitivities about homosexuality is to have a lot of people talk a great deal about the subject in a neutral or supportive way," is how Kirk and Madsen coached their acolytes. The "raw sensitivities" the gays seek to benumb are the hard-won experiences of millions of normal heterosexuals who have been menaced by a toxic encounter with a homosexual. The catastrophic ruin of countless lives due to the predations of homosexual Catholic priests only hints at the society-wide damage done by all homosexuals collectively. As I have demonstrated, homosexual males commit sex crimes at a rate **29 times** that of heterosexual males. The Boy Scouts of America wisely resists putting homosexuals into tents with boys because the Scouts has an encyclopedic logbook spanning decades that documents the sex crimes already committed by homosexuals who had penetrated the group's commonsense defenses. Of the 26,000 in-service sexual assaults that the Pentagon reported last year, 14,000 of them were male-on-male assaults. It's the Boy Scout scenario all over again. The uniforms are different, but the creepy behavior is the same.

Your task is to explain the manipulative nature of the gay agenda as frequently as possible – until everyone has heard the truth. The gays are hiding a lot. As the queer theorists told their troops: ". . . the masses should not be shocked and repelled by a premature exposure to homosexual behavior itself." That's because homosexual behavior is repellent to normal humans. When you talk of the manipulative gay agenda be sure to use the words of its gay authors who were trained psychologists and who understood that normal humans would be "shocked and repelled by . . . exposure to homosexual behavior itself."

"First let the camel get his nose inside the tent," crowed the Master Manipulators, "only later his unsightly derriere!" That's the authors of the gay agenda likening homosexual behaviors to a camel's ugly butt! Apparently, gays are only truthful when speaking to other gays.

You must shine a light on the gay tactic of pitting one church against another and one denomination against another, which is cynical and nasty. The gay manipulators cared nothing for the religious traditions or the future survival of religious communities; they sought nothing but the triumph of the homosexual sensibility. Their gay-activist acolytes are instructed that "When conservative churches condemn gays, there are only two things we can do to confound the homophobia of true believers. First, we can use talk to muddy the moral waters . . . Second, we can undermine the moral authority of homophobic churches by portraying them as antiquated backwaters, badly out of step with the times and with the latest findings of psychology."

That's the gay game plan: to "muddy the moral waters" and to "undermine the moral authority" of any church community that does not willingly toss Scripture into the dustbin of antiquated ideas. Traditionalists are to be ridiculed for being hopelessly *unfashionable* and "out of step" with the homosexual world vision. Churches that have no reservations about the radical

175

remodeling of America's moral landscape are to be used as battering rams and wrecking bars against those churches that cling to hard-won and time-honored wisdom.

Remember this: two of the most popular professions among homosexuals today are psychology and the clergy. After the American Psychiatric Association dropped homosexuality from its manual of disorders (using a junk-science mail ballot secretly funded and written by homosexual radicals) that group became a haven for homosexuals. Today the APA is a virtual gay-advocacy group. Likewise, a gay group working closely with the Episcopal Church estimates that one of every three Episcopal clergy is now a homosexual, which would make this church's moral pronouncements no more authoritative than those of any other gay-lesbian-bisexual-transgendered advocacy group.

The game plan is for gays to colonize a church with loose standards and then hollow it out by muddying the moral waters and then using the presumed moral authority of that church to weaken other churches that stand as a bulwark against a rising tide of weirdness.

The use of the words "homophobe" and "homophobic" are always slanders against the character of critics of the gay agenda. **Always** call attention to it! It is **hate** speech. These words are an attack on the critic, not a reasoned response to the critic's reasoned argument. People who use these words have no reasoned defense to offer; they have been reduced to throwing brickbats. The use of these words is intended to make everyone present believe that you are a pathologically hateful person. In truth, calling you a homophobe is no different than you calling a gay activist a faggot. It's an attack on the person; it is not a reasoned response to that person's argument. Liberals in the media have picked up this gay lingo; they now use these hate words casually as part of their everyday speech.

Remember this: It is not necessary for any of us to hate homosexuals in order to disagree with them about social policy. The homosexual agenda is not a threat to our culture because homosexuality is evil; it is a threat simply because the gay agenda is a remodeling of our moral and cultural matrix in ways that are problematic for the continuance of traditional heterosexual culture. This should be your principal talking point. Draw attention to their hate speech; demand a rational argument! Any person in the media who adopts the language of the radical gays must be identified as a foot soldier of the gay agenda. Letters of protest should follow after every use of the words "homophobe" or "homophobic" in any of our media because the use of this language is evidence that its user is a partisan of the gay agenda.

The gay mandate to "portray gays as victims, not as aggressive challengers" is an attempt to distract us from the documented history of homosexuals as amazing troublemakers. "A media campaign to promote the Gay Victim image should make use of symbols which reduce the mainstream's sense of threat, which lowers its guard and which enhances the plausibility of victimization," declared Kirk and Madsen.

Let's unpack this propaganda ploy. By "the mainstream's sense of threat" these gays mean the average person's suspicion of sexual behaviors that are very unusual. In the very next breath the queer theorists are instructing their minions to keep the "jaunty mustachioed musclemen" out of sight, to showcase harmless-looking old people, and that gay groups like NAMBLA "must play no part at all in such a campaign." In other words, **lie** to the normal folk for whom you have no respect whatsoever.

"Our campaign should not demand direct support of homosexual practices, should instead take anti-discrimination as its theme." By "discrimination" Madsen and Kirk do not mean "discerning judgment;" they mean prejudice. But ask yourself, is a cautious public *really* pre-judging homosexuals? Are the thousands of molested altar boys **pre-judging** the moral substance of the gay soul? Or is this generous sample of **experienced** heterosexual victims of gay predation **best** able to warn us of the consequences of an ever expanding homosexual comfort zone?

You must stress that homosexuals are not a minority as we commonly define a minority. Homosexuals do not share a common ethnicity; they do not share racial characteristics. There is no clearly identified cause of homosexuality; it may have many causes; it is always the result of some normal developmental process gone awry. In truth, we should refer to "homosexualities" in the plural. A collection of developmental oddities is not a genuine minority by any definition.

As I have demonstrated, numerous gays with Ph.D. degrees in psychology are openly contradicting the cornerstone claim of the gay agenda: that all homosexuals are "born that way." Many gays claim to be gay by choice.

The "Gay Rights" Scam

Take every opportunity to stress the fact that *everyone* has the same rights. Every adult male has the same right to marry the female of his choice and every adult female has the right to marry the male of her choice. Some people choose to **not** marry. Many gays **choose** to not marry because of their peculiar sexual predilections, but no homosexual is denied the right to marry. One of every five male homosexuals does marry a woman and one of every three lesbians marries a man. Everyone has the right to marry for whatever reason motivates them.

What homosexuals desire is the legalization of entirely new and *different* social institutions. These novel institutions are all about the emotional chemistries that are peculiar to lesbian and gay-male relationships. Homosexuals want the ninety-nine percent of us who are not homosexuals to pretend that their newly-created institutions are marriages *exactly like* traditional marriages. They are *desperate* for acceptance and legitimacy. Gays crave the borrowed luster of traditional heterosexual marriage, but the emotional echo chamber of same-sex pair bonding bears no resemblance to the nuanced romance of complementary heterosexual harmony.

The words "gay rights" are just a gay propagandist's term of art. What gays are seeking are **special privileges** tailor-made for homosexuals. The two new social institutions of one-sex wedlock are *special gay privileges* invented to gratify the 1% of our population who self-identify as homosexual.

The popular acceptance of "gay marriage" is not inevitable. Gays hang their hopes on opinion-poll returns that indicate that many young people (18 to 29) have no objections to homosexual wedlock; they see these young people as the gay-friendly voters of tomorrow. But polls also demonstrate that these same young people have wildly exaggerated notions of how many homosexuals actually exist. When these young people are asked how many gays there are in America they give answers as high as *25 or 30 percent!* The true number is closer to **one** percent.

There are several reasons to hope that the tide of public opinion has crested and will soon turn against the creation of marriage mutations. First of all, the average age of an American man's first marriage had risen to 28.9 years by the year 2011 and for women it had risen to 26.9 years. That's the *average* age of first marriages. For many career-oriented Americans it is even older. This means that the average American man or woman doesn't even *begin* to start taking marriage *seriously* until they are older than the group of 18-to-29-year-olds who are telling pollsters that novel marriage modalities don't trouble them.

A Pew poll in March of 2013 revealed that the softening of opposition to one-sex wedlock was driven by the young Millenials. Theirs was the **only** generation even to be *more likely* to favor one-sex wedlock more in 2013 than in 2012, as support from all other generations was declining. Support from Generation X has remained stagnant since 2001, stuck at 49 percent. Only among Millenials, who have been bombarded by slickly-crafted pro-gay propaganda since they were born, has support for mutant marriage modalities risen from 40 percent in 2003 to 70 percent in 2013. The good news is that the Millenials are not totally brainwashed.

A survey by the Berkley Center for Religion, Peace and World Affairs at Georgetown University, collaborating with the Public Religion Research Institute revealed that the Millenials "are nearly evenly divided over whether sex between two adults of the same gender is morally acceptable." This means that only about 35% of Millenials are highly resistant to reasonable persuasion by defenders of traditional human relations.

American youngsters have been bombarded by the gay narrative since birth. The popular media are awash with gay propaganda. Last night I watched an episode of Grey's Anatomy on television which included **five** lesbians in various relationships. For those five lesbians to be a truthful representation of the true proportion of lesbians to the rest of the American population that episode would have included close to **five hundred** named heterosexuals. The preposterous overrepresentation of homosexuals in the popular media is a favorite ploy of gay propagandists. These exaggerations give the false impression that gays are more than a tiny collection of behavioral curiosities.

Would these young people be as willing to legalize gay parodies of traditional marriage if they understood how few of the one percent who are homosexual would **ever** choose to marry? Remember: The average gay male pegs the number of his *different* sex partners at **five hundred!** Monogamy is **not** high on the list of gay values.

Never debate about specific gay couples. Most Americans don't care what people do in the privacy of their bedrooms; nobody wants to beat up on dear queer Bert and Ernie. We are engaged in a debate because the gay agenda has very **public** consequences that threaten our shared **public** culture. When "gay marriage" is used to *legitimize* homosexual behaviors and appetites in public forums, such as our churches and our public schools, then it is time to shine a white-hot spotlight on those behaviors.

Point One of the gay agenda is a call for gays to "desensitize" normal humans? The gays seek to blunt the moral sensibilities of ninety-nine percent of the American population. Madsen and Kirk used the word "benumb." That word alone should set off alarm

180

bells. The gay agenda reads like a revamp of the 50s sci-fi classic Invasion of the Body Snatchers. The gay aliens have arrived to "benumb" and "desensitize" normal humans.

The overwhelming majority of socialized humans have internalized the classical virtues of masculinity and femininity. Without these virtues a male is not a man and a female is not a woman as our culture defines man and woman. For men and women the music of their daily lives is a rich interweaving of gender counterpoint and harmony. The monotone drumbeat of one-sex relationships is a gender tone deafness that is alien to normal humans. Heterosexuals *experience* the effeminacy of gay males and the affected hardness of over-compensating lesbians as a boorish mockery of their *defining* heterosexual aesthetic. For billions of heterosexuals the world over the postures and poses of homosexuals are a *repudiation* of natural, species-sustaining, heterosexuality.

The queer theorists were careful to hide their intentions behind a veil of unthreatening blather about a need for "consistency" and "fair treatment." In their own words, "Our campaign should not demand direct support for homosexual practices . . ." Of course not! The puppet must never see the hand of the Puppet Master.

The homosexual counterculture coheres about appetites and perspectives that are deeply hostile to the values of heterosexual culture. There is no healthy way to "mainstream" a subculture in which the average gay male admits to having had 500 different sex partners, most of them anonymous strangers. If heterosexuals behaved as homosexuals do, the American economy would have collapsed in the wake of a heterosexual AIDS epidemic. That didn't happen because the values of heterosexual culture are a firewall against wildfire STD contagion. In any case, there is no possible way to domesticate *an entire subculture* of these randy gay satyrs. They could not be "mainstreamed."

The gay agenda is all about how to "Make gays look good." This has been a media theme for the last three decades. Ask yourself, have you *ever* seen a **nasty** homosexual character in any television

181

drama, stage play, movie or news broadcast in the last thirty years? If you are younger that thirty your answer is definitely "No" because you have been a captive of the gay-agenda bubble for all of your life. Homosexual predator clergy are instantly re-branded as "pedophile priests" to distance them from their gay brethren; stories about homicidal homosexual rapists are mysteriously deemed to be "not news" by the liberal media. Every newscast has been sanitized by the self-appointed defenders of the gay social agenda.

When Matthew Shepard was murdered the media were united in their slant that he had been killed by gay-hating heterosexuals. Only later, *much* later, did a single broadcast reveal that Matthew Shepard had been killed to conceal a previous sexual relationship between Shepard and his killer. Shepard's killer was a closeted homosexual.

At that same time the breaking news that two homosexuals had kidnapped, drugged, raped and murdered young Jesse Dirkhising was deemed to be "not news" by the liberal media. The story never got farther than a few local news spots. Clearly, the liberal media are carrying water for the homosexual sub-culture. Clearly, the life of Matthew Shepard was valued more highly than the life of Jesse Dirkhising by the doctrinaire liberals at ABC, NBC, CBS, MSNBC, *The Washington Post*, *The New York Times*, *The Baltimore Sun*, *Newsweek*, *Time* and all the rest of the gay-agenda handmaidens.

Our mission as defenders of traditional marriage is to speak the truth to Powerful Liberal Media. America's print and visual media, collectively, are our public forums; our voices should be heard in all of those forums – loudly and clearly.

The published gay agenda calls on gay activists and their liberal fellow travelers in the media to "Make the victimizers look bad." By "victimizers" Kirk and Madsen mean any and all critics of the gay game plan. They speak of their intent to replace the preference that normal humans have for normal human behaviors with feelings of "shame and guilt."

"At a later stage of the media campaign . . . it will be time to get tough with remaining opponents," declared Madsen and Kirk. "To be blunt, they must be vilified." In other words, all normal people must be made to experience "shame and guilt" as punishments for clinging to the traditional values that have preserved human cultures for millennia. The know-it-all gays have appointed themselves to be our disciplinarians. The fact that every life-enhancing human culture was created to accommodate the complementary dispositions of the ninety-nine percent of humanity who successfully progress to robust heterosexuality is a truth totally lost on homosexuals. To their gay way of thinking this commonsense recognition of normal Human Nature is evidence of an unhealthy "homophobia" that is deserving of punishing "shame and guilt." The gays propose a campaign of vilification; they call for a campaign of divide-and-conquer, pitting one church against another.

The Cost of Saving Our Culture

The authors of the gay agenda believed that gays were a goldmine "because those gays not supporting families usually have more discretionary income than average, they could afford to contribute much more." And they have. Though only one in a hundred Americans is a homosexual, *one in six* of President Obama's big-bucks bundlers is gay; homosexuals appear **sixteen times** more frequently among Obama's inner circle than in the general population.

Homosexual carpetbaggers now win votes for "gay marriage" by flooding far-away election contests with previously-unheard-of amounts of campaign cash to bolster the candidates of their choice. Money pours in from Hollywood to finance the obliteration of traditional candidates thousands of miles away. The local voters don't know what hit them; they are swamped by negative advisements smearing the candidate who best represents their values. It's the gay way of disenfranchising traditional Americans. A fund to neutralize this crooked gay practice would be a firewall against gays who use their "discretionary income" to purchase candidates and thwart the will of the normal majority.

The defenders of normalcy must make the preservation of our heterosexual culture their first priority. It's a fact that conservatives are far more generous than liberals; numerous polls demonstrate that the most liberal people are also the stingiest. Therefore, to adequately fund the defense of traditional marriage all that needs to be done is for the millions of generous traditional Americans to **redirect** their charitable dollars to groups that are dedicated to defending traditional folkways and values.

The charitable organizations of America are overwhelmingly administered by liberals, but these same charities are overwhelmingly **funded** by conservative donors. It would be a chastising comeuppance for these self-satisfied liberal administrators to suffer abrupt financial setbacks as millions of traditional Americans choose to divert their contributions to causes more local and personal – such as the preservation of traditional marriage in America. Conservatives in America outnumber liberals by a margin of more than two to one; it's high time that our traditional vision of healthy normalcy was the dominant vision shaping America's future. We are the Normal Majority. We hold the power to preserve our life-enhancing civilization.

Please share this book with friends and clergy. It is a handbook for social change.

28103230R00109

Made in the USA
Charleston, SC
31 March 2014